OUT & ABOUT

• WALKING GUIDES TO BRITAIN •

No 9

South Wales

From 1 April 1996, local authority boundaries in Wales will change.
For up-to-date information, contact the Local Government Reorganisation
Section of the Welsh Office on (01222) 825 111.

First published in Great Britain in 1996 by
Marshall Cavendish Books, London
(a division of Marshall Cavendish Partworks Ltd)

Copyright © 1996 Marshall Cavendish

ISBN 0319 00580 1

British Library Cataloguing in Publication Data:
A catalogue record for this book is available from the British Library

Printed and bound in Malaysia

Some of this material has previously appeared in the Marshall Cavendish partwork OUT & ABOUT

CONTENTS

4 Introduction

Gwent

11 **1** Into the Black Mountains • *15* **2** The Blorenge Mountain

19 **3** Llanthony Priory • *23* **4** The 365 Steps • *25* **5** Boulder and Boulder

27 **6** Follies and Forts • *31* **7** Along the Canal at Pontypool • *33* **8** Above the Wye Valley

35 **9** On the Wye Gorge • *37* **10** Ruins and Renovations

41 **11** Marching through the Marches

Mid Glamorgan

45 **12** Guto's Grave • *47* **13** Garth Hill

49 **14** The Castle by the Dunes • *51* **15** From Collieries to Country Park

South Glamorgan

55 **16** Prince Silian's Cave • *57* **17** The Fairy-Tale Castle • *59* **18** A Castle and Cliffs

61 **19** Waves Across the Waves

West Glamorgan

63 **20** Rhossili Bay • *65* **21** Aberdulais Falls

69 **22** Caves and Coves • *71* **23** The Talbots of Margam

Dyfed

73 **24** Bosherston Ponds • *75* **25** The Sound of the Sea

77 **26** North of Aberystwyth • *79* **27** Home of the Eisteddfod

83 **28** Across the Sands at Ynyslas • *85* **29** Coastline of Shipwrecks • *87* **30** A Savage Coast

91 **31** The Golden Road • *95* **32** An Elegant Resort • *97* **33** A Smugglers' Cove

99 **34** The Gwaun Valley • *101* **35** Lakes and Cliffs • *103* **36** Sampson's Stone

105 **37** Gerald's Castle • *109* **38** The Castle on the Rock • *111* **39** The Poet and the Castles

115 **40** The College on the Dulas • *117* **41** Land of the White Canons

119 **42** A Walk through Wild Wales • *123* **43** Above the Teifi

125 Index

Introduction to

OUT & ABOUT

• WALKING GUIDES TO BRITAIN •

Walking has become one of the most popular pastimes in Britain. To enjoy walking, you don't need any special skills, you don't have to follow rules or join expensive clubs, and you don't need any special equipment – though a pair of walking boots is a good idea! It is an easy way of relaxing and getting some exercise, and of enjoying nature and the changing seasons.

The OUT & ABOUT WALKING GUIDES TO BRITAIN will give you ideas for walks in your own neighbourhood and in other areas of Britain. All the walks are devised around a theme and range in length from about 2 to 9 miles (3.25 to 14.5 km) and in difficulty from very easy to mildly strenuous. Since each walk is circular, you will always be able to get back to your starting point.

Devised by experts and tested for accuracy, all the walks are accompanied by clear, practical instructions and an enlarged section of the relevant Ordnance Survey map. The flavour of the walk and highlights to look out for are described in the introductory text.

LOCAL COLOUR

Background features give you extra insight into items of local interest. The OUT & ABOUT WALKING GUIDES TO BRITAIN relate legends, point out unusual architectural details, provide a potted history of the lives of famous writers and artists connected with a particular place, explain traditional crafts still practised by local artisans, and uncover the secrets behind an ever-changing landscape.

DISCOVER NATURE

One of the greatest pleasures in going for a walk is the sense of being close to nature. On the walks suggested in the OUT & ABOUT WALKING GUIDES TO BRITAIN, you can feel the wind, smell the pine trees, hear the birds and see the beauty of the countryside. You will become more aware of the seasons – the life cycles of butterflies, the mating calls of birds, the protective behaviour of all creatures with their young. You will see the beginning of new life in the forests and fields, the bluebell carpets in spring woodlands, the dazzling beauty of rhododendron bushes in early summer, the swaying cornfields of summer and the golden colours of leaves in autumn. The OUT & ABOUT WALKING GUIDES TO BRITAIN tell you what to look out for and where to find it.

NATURE WALK

Occasional nature walk panels will highlight an interesting feature that you will see on your walk. You will learn about natural and manmade details in the landscape, how to tell which animal or bird has nibbled the cones in a pine forest, what nurse trees are and what a triangulation point is.

ABOVE: *Colourful narrowboats are always an attractive feature on inland waterways.*

route refer you to the numbered stages in the written directions. In addition, points of interest are marked on the maps with letters. Each one is mentioned in the walk directions and is described in detail in the introductory text.

COUNTRYWISE

The countryside is one of our greatest resources. If we treat it with respect, we can preserve it for the future.

Throughout the countryside there is a network of paths and byways. Some are former trading routes, others are simply the paths villagers took to visit one another in the days before public transport. Most are designated 'rights of way': footpaths, open only to people on foot, and bridleways, open to people on foot, horseback or bicycle. These paths can be identified on Ordnance Survey maps and verified, in cases of dispute, by the definitive map for the area, held by the relevant local authority.

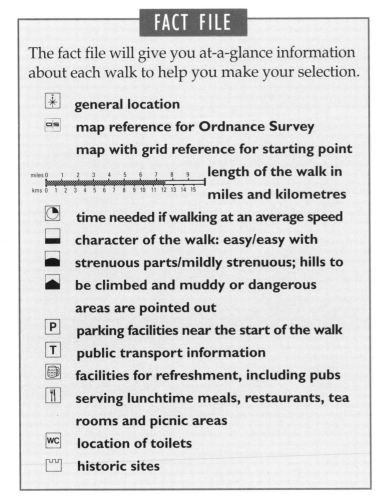

THE LAW OF TRESPASS

If you find a public right of way barred to you, you may remove the obstruction or take a short detour around it. However, in England and Wales, if you stray from the footpath you are trespassing and could be sued in a civil court for damages. In Scotland, rights of way are not recorded on definitive maps, nor is there a law of trespass. Although you may cross mountain and moorland paths, landowners are permitted to impose restrictions on access, such as during the grouse-shooting season, which should be obeyed.

If you are following a public right of way and find, for example, that your path is blocked by a field of crops, you are entitled to walk the line of the footpath through the crops, in single file. Farmers are required, by law, to restore public rights of way within 14 days of ploughing. However, if you feel uncomfortable about doing this and can find a way round, then do so. But report the matter to the local authority who will take the necessary action to clear the correct route.

RIGHT: *The stunning patchwork of fields surrounding the picturesque village of Widecombe in the heart of Dartmoor makes a beautiful setting for the famous annual fair.*
BELOW: *Brown hares boxing in spring are a fascinating sight.*

It is illegal for farmers to place a bull on its own in a field crossed by a right of way (unless the bull is not a recognized dairy breed). If you come across a bull alone in a field, find another way round.

COMMONS AND PARKS

There are certain areas in England and Wales where you may be able to wander without keeping to paths, such as most commons and beaches. There are also country parks, set up by local authorities for public recreation – parkland, woodland, heath or farmland.

The National Trust is the largest private landowner in England and Wales. Its purpose is to preserve areas of natural beauty and sites of historic interest by acquisition, holding them in trust for public access and enjoyment. Information on access may be obtained from National Trust headquarters at

THE COUNTRY CODE

- ■ **Enjoy the countryside, and respect its life and work**

- ■ **Always guard against risk of fire**

- ■ **Fasten all gates**

- ■ **Keep your dogs under close control**

- ■ **Keep to public footpaths across farmland**

- ■ **Use gates and stiles to cross fences, hedges and walls**

- ■ **Leave livestock, crops and machinery alone**

- ■ **Take your litter home**

- ■ **Help to keep all water clean**

- ■ **Protect wildlife, plants and trees**

- ■ **Take special care on country roads**

- ■ **Make no unnecessary noise**

36 QueenAnne's Gate, London SW1H 9AS
Tel: 0171-222 9251.

ABOVE RIGHT *Carelessness with cigarettes, matches or camp fires can be devastating in a forest.*

Most regions of great scenic beauty in England and Wales are designated National Parks or Areas of Outstanding Natural Beauty (AONB). In Scotland, they are known as National Scenic Areas (NSAs) or AONBs.

Most of this land is privately owned and there is no right of public access. In some cases, local authorities may have negotiated agreements with landowners to allow walkers access on mountains and moors.

CONSERVATION

National park, AONB or NSA status is intended to provide some measure of protection for the land-scape, guarding against unsuitable development while encouraging enjoyment of its natural beauty.

Nature reserves are areas set aside for conservation. Most are privately owned, some by large organizations such as the Royal Society for the Protection of Birds. Although some offer public access, most require permission to enter.

THE RAMBLERS ASSOCIATION

The aims of the Ramblers Association are to further greater understanding and care of the countryside, to protect and enhance public rights of way and areas of natural beauty, to improve public access to the countryside, and to encourage more people to take up rambling as a healthy, recreational activity. It has played an important role in preserving and developing our national footpath network.

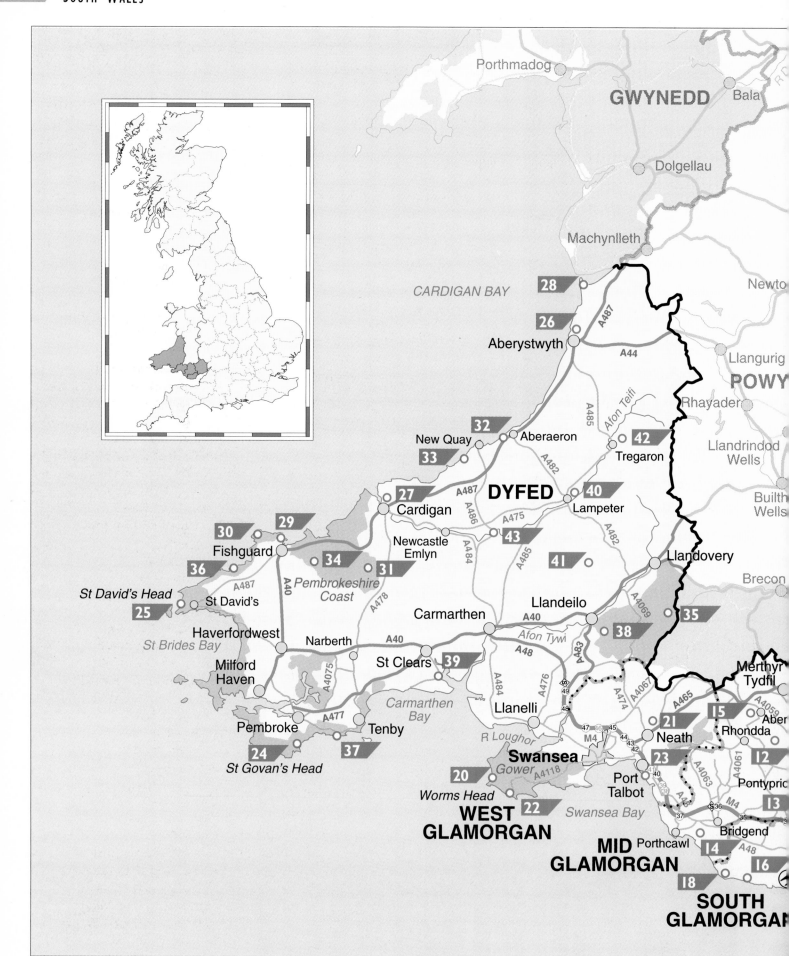

Porthmadog

GWYNEDD Bala

Dolgellau

Machynlleth

CARDIGAN BAY

28

26 A487

Aberystwyth A44

Newto

Llangurig

POWY

A485 Afon Teifi

Rhayader

32

New Quay Aberaeron

33

42

Tregaron

Llandrindod
Wells

27 A487

DYFED

A482

40

Lampeter

Builth
Wells

Cardigan

A486

A475

30 29

Fishguard

36

St David's Head

25

St David's

34

A487 Pembrokeshire
Coast

31

A40

A478

43

A484

A485

41

Llandovery

Brecon

St Brides Bay

Haverfordwest

Narberth

A40

Newcastle
Emlyn

Carmarthen

Llandeilo

A40

38 A4069

35

Afon Tywi

A48

A83

A4067

Milford
Haven

A4075

St Clears

39

A484

A476

A474

Merthyr
Tydfil

A465

15 A4059

Aber

Rhondda

12

A477

Carmarthen
Bay

Llanelli

47 46 45

M4

44

43

42

23 A40

A4063

49

48

21

Neath

Pembroke

Tenby

R Loughor

A4061

Pontypric

24

St Govan's Head

37

20

Worms Head

Swansea

Gower A4118

Port
Talbot

A48

S36

35

M4

13

WEST
GLAMORGAN

22

Swansea Bay

14 A48

Bridgend

MID
GLAMORGAN Porthcawl

18

16

SOUTH
GLAMORGAN

South Wales

All the walks featured in this book are plotted and numbered on the regional map (left) and listed in the box below.

1	**Into the Black Mountains**
2	**The Blorenge Mountain**
3	**Llanthony Priory**
4	**The 365 Steps**
5	**Boulder and Boulder**
6	**Follies and Forts**
7	**Along the Canal at Pontypool**
8	**Above the Wye Valley**
9	**On the Wye Gorge**
10	**Ruins and Renovations**
11	**Marching through the Marches**
12	**Guto's Grave**
13	**Garth Hill**
14	**The Castle by the Dunes**
15	**From Collieries to Country Park**
16	**Prince Silian's Cave**
17	**The Fairy-Tale Castle**
18	**A Castle and Cliffs**
19	**Waves Across the Waves**
20	**Rhossili Bay**
21	**Aberdulais Falls**
22	**Caves and Coves**
23	**The Talbots of Margam**
24	**Bosherston Ponds**
25	**The Sound of the Sea**
26	**North of Aberystwyth**
27	**Home of the Eisteddfod**
28	**Across the Sands at Ynyslas**
29	**Coastline of Shipwrecks**
30	**A Savage Coast**
31	**The Golden Road**
32	**An Elegant Resort**
33	**A Smugglers' Cove**
34	**The Gwaun Valley**
35	**Lakes and Cliffs**
36	**Sampson's Stone**
37	**Gerald's Castle**
38	**The Castle on the Rock**
39	**The Poet and the Castles**
40	**The College on the Dulas**
41	**Land of the White Canons**
42	**A Walk through Wild Wales**
43	**Above the Teifi**

USING MAPS

Although the OUT & ABOUT WALKING GUIDES TO BRITAIN give you all the information you need, it is useful to have some basic map skills. Most of us have some experience of using a motoring atlas to navigate by car. Navigating when walking is much the same, except that mistakes are much more time and energy consuming and, if circumstances conspire, could lead to an accident.

A large-scale map is the answer to identifying where you are. Britain is fortunate in having the best mapping agency in the world, the Ordnance Survey, which produces high-quality maps, the most popular being the 1:50,000 Landranger series. However, the most useful for walkers are the 1:25,000 Pathfinder, Explorer and Outdoor Leisure maps.

THE LIE OF THE LAND

A map provides more than just a bird's eye view of the land; it also conveys information about the terrain – whether marshy, forested, covered with tussocky grass or boulders; it distinguishes between footpaths and bridleways; and shows boundaries such as parish and county boundaries.

Symbols are used to identify a variety of landmarks such as churches, camp and caravan sites, bus, coach and rail stations, castles, caves and historic houses. Perhaps most importantly of all, the shape of the land is indicated by contour lines. Each line represents land at a specific height so it is possible to read the gradient from the spacing of the lines (the closer the spacing, the steeper the hill).

GRID REFERENCES

All Ordnance Survey maps are overprinted with a framework of squares known as the National Grid. This is a reference system which, by breaking the country down into squares, allows you to pinpoint any place in the country and give it a unique reference number; very useful when making rendezvous arrangements. On OS Landranger, Pathfinder and Outdoor Leisure maps it is possible to give a reference to an accuarcy of 100 metres. Grid squares on these maps cover an area of 1 km x 1 km on the ground.

GIVING A GRID REFERENCE

Blenheim Palace in Oxfordshire has a grid reference of **SP 441 161.** This is constructed as follows:
  SP These letters identify the 100 km grid square in which Blenheim Palace lies. These squares form the basis of the National Grid. Information on the

100 km square covering a particular map is always given in the map key.
  441 161 This six figure reference locates the position of Blenheim Palace to 100 metres in the 100 km grid square.
  44 This part of the reference is the number of the grid line which forms the western (left-hand) boundary of the 1 km grid square in which Blenheim Palace appears. This number is printed in the top and bottom margins of the relevant OS map (Pathfinder 1092 in this case).
  16 This part of the reference is the number of the grid line which forms the southern (lower) boundary of the 1 km grid square in which Blenheim Palace appears. This number is printed in the left- and right-hand margins of the relevant OS map (Pathfinder 1092).
  These two numbers together (SP 4416) locate the bottom left-hand corner of

the 1 km grid square in which Blenheim Palace appears. The remaining figures in the reference **441 161** pinpoint the position within that square by dividing its western boundary lines into tenths and estimating on which imaginary tenths line Blenheim Palace lies.

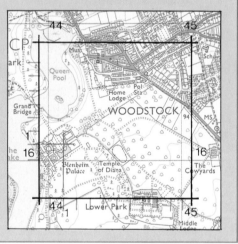

INTO THE BLACK MOUNTAINS

I

A visit to two ancient churches hidden in the mountains

In the very heart of the Black Mountains lies the remote Grwyne Fawr valley, where the walk begins. Woods, rivers and streams abound, and the route climbs up to ridges which give some excellent views of the hills and valleys. The highlight of the walk is visiting two little churches dating back to medieval times, each with something unique to offer.

The entrance to the valley is at Fforest Coal Pit **Ⓐ**. This hamlet takes its name not from a coal mine, but from the wooded nature of the valley and the fact that charcoal burning took place here.

THE BISHOP'S BRIDGE

Not long after the start, you cross the ancient packhorse bridge **Ⓑ** known as Pont Escob (the Bishop's Bridge). It is named after Archbishop Baldwin who came this way in 1188 while on a tour of Wales to recruit men to fight in the Holy Land on the Third Crusade.

FACT FILE

✳ Fforest Coal Pit, Brecon Beacons National Park, Wales

🗺 Outdoor Leisure Map 13, grid reference SO 285211

miles 0 1 2 3 4 5 6 7 8 9 10 miles
kms 0 1 2 3 4 5 6 7 8 9 10 11 12 13 14 15 kms

🕐 Allow 5 hours

▬ A varied walk involving three steep but fairly short ascents. Bridle path may be muddy in wet weather. Walking boots are recommended

P Drive north of Abergavenny via Bettws to Fforest Coal Pit. Park by a telephone box at the entrance to the Grwyne Fawr valley

🍴 No facilities en route. The Queen's Head Inn is ½ mile (800 metres) south along the road from the point where it is crossed by the walk near Cwmyoy village hall. It can be reached by a detour on the walk, or by car afterwards

WC

▲ *The village of Cwmyoy in the Black Mountains. The name 'Cwmyoy' means 'Valley of the Yoke', a reference to the shape of the hillside above the church (inset). This little medieval church is leaning due to subsidence.*

▼ *Lush hedgerows edge the road beyond Partrishow Church.*

THE WALK

FFOREST COAL PIT-PARTRISHOW-CWMYOY

*This walk starts from Fforest Coal Pit **A** at the entrance to the Grwyne Fawr valley. Park in the road near a telephone box.*

1 From the telephone box go back down the road a short way to reach a crossroads and take the first turning on the right. This leads to a humped-back stone bridge known as Pont Escob, or the Bishop's Bridge **B**. From here continue up the hill to a T-junction and turn right.

2 A steep ascent leads to another road junction. Keep to the right and follow the road which soon levels out, around the hillside to reach the Nant Mair Valley. The church of Partrishow **D** will be seen on the other side of the valley.

3 Descend to a hairpin bend in the valley where some steps lead down to the historic Holy Well of St Patricio **C**. After having had a look at the well, continue up the road which now steepens again, to reach the lych gate of the church on the right.

4 After visiting the church, go through a gate at the other end of the churchyard and follow a path through the fields to reach a track descending through a gate past an old farmhouse which is called Twyn-y-Llwyn.

5 Just after the farmhouse turn left through a gate and cross a field to a waymarked gate and stile. Bear right down through the next field to another waymarked gate. Go diagonally left to pass between two ruined buildings and follow the track down to a stile in a fence above the Grwyne Fawr road. Cross the road to follow a lane opposite, which crosses the river on a bridge and passes the Tabernacle Baptist Chapel.

6 Continue up the lane, ascending the side of the ridge to a gate where the track forks. Take the right fork up to a barn and then make a sharp turn to the right. Head up the track towards the ridge which first has trees and then a wall on the right and arrive at a gate in a stone wall with a walled rectangular field enclosure ahead left. Go left and then right to ascend beside the left wall of the enclosure and shortly reach the ridge crest track. Turn right along the ridge for about 100 yards (90 metres), then turn off left through a gate and follow a path down to a gap in a stone wall.

7 Go through a hunting gate and enter a forestry plantation. Follow a stony path down through the trees to reach a forest road. Turn left and then immediately right to follow a continuation of the previous path down through a second hunting gate.

8 Go through the next hunting gate and the path bears to the right and goes down through a tunnel of trees to reach a road. Watch out for traffic (be careful here) and then go straight across the road and cross over a stile.

9 After crossing a field, go over a stile at the corner of a bridge. Turn right and very shortly go over a stile on the right. Head diagonally left to cross a ditch and a stile. Within about 20 yards (18 metres), go up a rising track on the left close to a hedge to a fine old slab stile to a road. Go right up the road and shortly left up a track leading directly up to Cwmyoy Church **E** via a kissing gate.

10 Having visited this church, walk through the churchyard and follow the road down to a telephone box and Cwmyoy Farm. Turn left and after about 150 yards (135 metres) turn right by a gate/footpath sign. Keeping the hedge on your right, follow the edge of a field and go through the trees directly ahead to reach a footbridge spanning the River Honddu.

11 Carry straight on for about 50 yards (45 metres) and then turn right up a rutted track leading to a stile. Cross the next field to reach another stile near the village hall. With care, cross the road and go over a stile on the other side. Follow a track up to a farm and then turn left beside a stone wall to reach a stile in a fence. Continue through the trees, following a broad track. Cross a forestry track and go up the diagonal path on the other side.

12 On reaching a road, go straight across and follow a broad cart track beside a fence. It contours around the hillside providing excellent views. After passing through a gate it leads down through more gates to join a road. Turn left and then follow the road down to reach the crossroads which lie near to the start of the walk.

The greater spotted, or pied, woodpecker, can be heard 'drumming' away on the wooded hillsides.

Situated in the sheltered valley of Nant Mair (Mary's Brook) lies a little stone-covered well commemorating St Patricio **C**. His name, anglicised to Partrishow, has been given to the surrounding area. Near here, the holy man built a simple cell and one day he gave shelter to a traveller who repaid his kindness by murdering him. Some years later a rich pilgrim suffering from leprosy came here seeking a cure. The holy water did the trick and he left a hatful of gold for a church to be built. An inscribed cross on a stone just above the well marks the spot where Archbishop Baldwin stood to preach to the local people.

A LONELY CHURCH

The Church of Partrishow **D** stands alone — there is no surrounding village. It dates back to 1060 and in the 13th century the chancel and west chapel were added. Its greatest treasure is a beautiful 15th-century rood screen, carved from Irish oak. The intricate designs

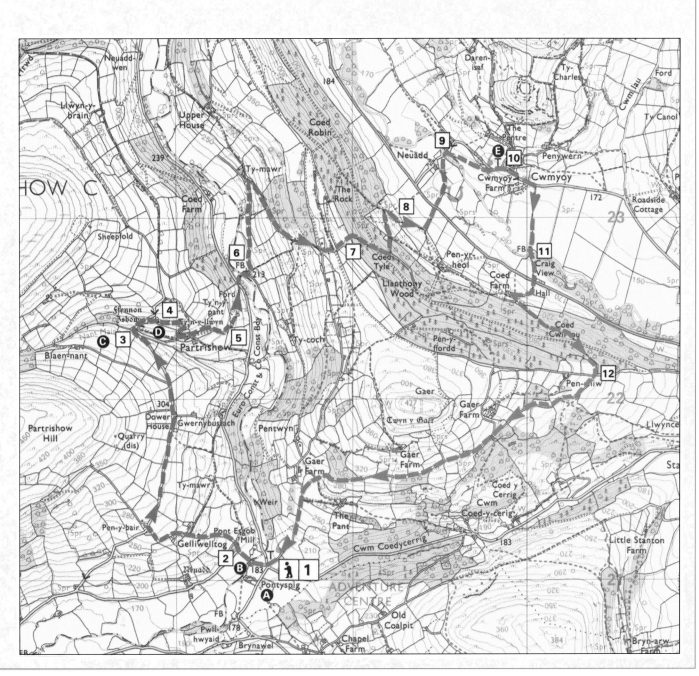

include the dragon as a symbol of evil, devouring a vine which represents goodness. On the west wall is a gruesome 'Doom' figure — a skeleton holding a scythe, spade and hourglass to remind the visitor that the Day of Judgement is drawing near.

Another unusual church is found at Cwmyoy **E**, clinging to the hillside at a perilous angle. When you enter it, the effect is very disconcerting, destroying any sense

The isolated church at Partrishow was founded in the 11th century.

of balance. Its tilt is caused by **subsidence** of the foundations over the centuries.

This part of the Black Mountains is Old Red Sandstone which on high ground breaks down into a limeless soil supporting bilberries and heather. Mountain ash covers the hills and its berries provide food for the ring ouzel. Other birds to be seen in the area are kestrels, buzzards, peewits and skylarks.

▲ *The 'Doom' figure in Partrishow Church is to remind visitors of death. (above left) The intricately carved gallery above the rood screen in the same church.*
◄ *Horseshoe bats asleep. These bats are gregarious and noisy. They breed in roofs and hibernate in caves or mines.*

The Charcoal Burner

Charcoal burning was once an important rural industry and charcoal was used for glass-making and iron-smelting. To make charcoal, wood is burnt very slowly, with insufficient oxygen to make it burn properly. The complete process takes up to a week and during that time the charcoal burner lives in a tent by his fire for he must keep an eye on it at all times.

He uses lengths of 'cordwood' — off-cuts that the woodcutters have left for him. On the first day he makes his kiln, marking out a circle of 25 feet (7.5 metres) and erecting a vertical chimney of logs in the centre. Round this he builds up a pile of wood 6 feet (2 metres) high, and covers it with turf, and then earth. The chimney in the centre is clear and the fire is lit by tipping burning charcoal down it. The chimney is then sealed with a lead lid and covered with earth.

The charcoal burner now has to watch his smouldering mound very carefully, day and night, for it has to be tended every couple of hours. He may use a screen to keep off the wind. If the wood appears to be burning more fiercely in one part of the mound then this has to be covered with soil. It is essential that the fire burns very slowly and evenly.

Gradually the pile sinks and finally burns itself out. It is then ready to be opened. The hard black sticks of charcoal are raked out and put into sacks for collection. A ton of wood yields about 2 cwt (102 kg) of charcoal. Today, the change to coal has led to a decline in the demand for charcoal.

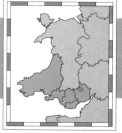

Alongside a canal cut into the mountain

This is a route which combines a hill walk that offers truly spectacular views with an intriguing look at transport routes of two centuries ago.

Even from the start, at the car park, there is an indication of the spectacular views of the Usk Valley and the surrounding countryside that are to be enjoyed from the slopes of Blorenge. For the first part of the walk, however, the view is closed in by trees that overhang the footpath and later the road, during the steep descent to the Brecon and Abergavenny Canal.

This canal, which was begun in 1799, links Brecon to Pontypool and is a most beautiful waterway running through the Brecon Beacons National Park. It runs on a narrow ledge cut into the hillside, following the natural contours of the land. The hillside above the waterway is heavily wooded, with mature trees leaning over the canal, and is home to a variety of woodland birds and grey squirrels. The water of the canal itself is full of fish, and shoals

◀ *The warehouse and loading wharf at Llanfoist is on the lovely Brecon and Abergavenny Canal (above, left and below), an isolated canal unconnected to the rest of the nationwide canal system. The whinchat (inset) inhabits the uplands, hiding its nest in the bracken-covered hillside.*

FACT FILE

* ✳ Blorenge, Brecon Beacons National Park .

* 🚉 Pathfinder 1086 (SO 21/31), grid reference SO 285109

  miles 0   1   2   3   4   5   6   7   8   9   10 miles
  kms 0   1 2 3 4 5 6 7 8 9 10   11 12 13 14 15 kms

* 🕐 Allow 3½ hours

* ◣ Steep and rough in places, so good walking shoes are recommended

* Ⓟ Large car park on minor road on south side of Blorenge

* 🍴 Refreshments and toilets at Govilon

The road on the Blorenge Mountain near the beginning of the walk.

of roach and large carp are often to be seen.

Below the Brecon and Abergavenny Canal, the hillside drops away steeply to the Usk Valley. The canal was for many years derelict but, following its restoration in 1964, pleasure boats now travel on it.

The most interesting place is Llanfoist ❶. It is here that trucks were lowered down the steep hill loaded with pig iron from the works at Blaenavon and stored in the warehouse under the canal. The barges could float in underneath for direct loading. The trucks could also cross the canal on the wooden bridge, and there is a pedestrian tunnel under the canal.

Along the way, there are places where the canal narrows. Here a section of canal could be isolated by dropping planks into grooves or by swinging a gate across the gap. This enabled workmen to drain that stretch of the canal so that maintenance work could be carried out.

The next big wharf is at Govilon ❷, now used for pleasure boats. The working boats were 55 feet (16.5 metres) long and the wide section here, known as a 'winding hole', allowed them space to turn round.

MOVING HEAVY CARGO

Two hundred years ago, canals were to the world of industry what motorways and railways are today — the major routes for moving heavy cargoes around the country. A single horse pulling a cart along even the best roads of the time could move no more than a two ton(ne) load; the same horse hauling a boat along the still waters of a canal could shift as much as 50 tons (49.2 tonnes) at a time.

Today, walking along the tree-shaded towpath of the Brecon and Abergavenny Canal, it is hard to see this as a vital link in a transport system serving major industrial complexes, but this is just what it was. It carried stone from quarries in the hills, coal from the local mines and iron from the foundries. It linked in directly to the Monmouthshire Canal, which led, in turn, to the docks at Cardiff. So when walking the towpath, imagine it as it was at the beginning of the 19th century, when horses, not walkers, used the path, pulling behind them the heavily laden boats.

On leaving the canal, the walk briefly joins the trackbed of an old railway. This was the Merthyr, Tredegar and Abergavenny Railway, begun in 1859. Among its promoters were the Hill family, who had built the old tramway to

▲ *A view of the north side of the Blorenge Mountain from the banks of the River Usk.*

◄ *Looking down from the heights of the mountain on to the busy market town of Abergavenny.*

Llanfoist half a century before.

Making the steep climb up from Govilon is rewarded by a level walk with superb views. This flat grassy track ❸ has rows of square stones, many with circular holes in the centre. This shows it to be an old 'tramway', an early form of railway where the trucks were hauled by horses. The stones are the original

THE WALK

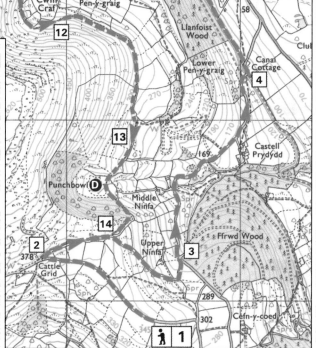

LLANFOIST — GOVILON

The walk begins at Little Cefn-y-coed Roadside Rest. From Blaenavon, take the B4246 and, after about 1 mile (1.6 km), turn right along the single track road that begins by the National Park boundary stone. There are three official parking places on this road: the walk starts at the third.

1 Standing at the car park, facing the road, turn right up the hill.

2 Immediately beyond the cattle grid, turn right on to the bridleway by the sign reading 'Llanfoist 3.2 km'. Continue on past the woodland and straight ahead down the path between the stone wall and the wire fence. The path continues downhill along a gulley overhung by massive trees. It is often easier walking on the rim of the gulley, but please note that all the gates are in the gulley itself.

3 At the road, turn left and follow the narrow road downhill.

4 Cross the bridge over the canal, and climb over the stile at the right-hand side to join the towpath. Turn right to go back under the bridge. After ⅔ mile (1 km), you pass Llanfoist wharf **A**.

5 At the first stone bridge, continue on the towpath by crossing the bridge and carry on to Govilon wharf **B**.

6 At the far end of Govilon wharf, beyond Bridge No. 97, is a 'skew' bridge crossing the canal at an angle. Climb the steps up from the towpath to reach the old railway line. Turn left.

7 Cross the stile by the former level crossing cottage to join the road. Turn left and immediately right at the T-junction. Follow the higher of the two roads, Cwm Road, leaving the large hollow oak tree on your right.

8 At the T-junction turn left uphill at The Old Schoolhouse at Cwm Lane.

9 Turn left immediately beyond the whitewashed house, Mount Pleasant, on to rough track.

10 At top of the wide track continue straight on through the little gate on to the narrow, rough footpath.

11 Cross straight over the road, and follow the footpath by the wood, signposted 'Llanfoist 2.5 km'. Beyond the first two stiles, follow the left-hand wall alongside the wood and look for uphill path through the ferns after the third stile. Follow this path to join a broad, flat grassy track **C**. Turn to your left and follow this old tramway to join a fence interspersed with wall to the left. Follow the wall.

12 Where the wall turns downhill, keep to the same level as indicated by yellow arrow on a stone to join the well-trodden path downhill.

13 The path brings you to a stile. Do not cross the stile, but turn right to follow the grassy track through the bracken. Keeping the hedge to the left, walk straight ahead. Enter the Punchbowl **D** after passing through the third gate.

14 Keeping the pool of water to the right, follow track uphill to the gulley followed on outward journey. Return along the gulley to the road and further on to the car park.

The Beginning of a Transport System

The canal is built in difficult, hilly countryside, but manages to keep to a level by hugging the hillside and following the natural contours of the land. Even so, the main customers, such as the quarries in the hills and the iron works of Blaenavon on the far side of the Blorenge, were still inaccessible by water. So these had to be joined to the canal by a network of tramways — railways built in the age before the steam locomotive had been invented.

The railway trucks, like the canal boats, had to be pulled by horses. But it would have been impossible for a horse to pick its way down a modern railway track where the rails are carried on sleepers. So these early railways were mounted on square, stone blocks sunk into the ground, leaving a clear space between the rails for the horse to walk. Lines of these old stone sleepers can be seen along the walk.

Even the combination of railway and canal was not sufficient. The grassy track that the walk follows, high on Blorenge, was a tramway built by the Hill family who controlled the iron works at Blaenavon. It was completed by 1820, but there was still the problem of connecting the two routes. This was achieved by 'inclined planes'. Loaded trucks were dropped down a track on the hillside, fastened to a continuous cable controlled by a brake drum. The weight of the loaded trucks was used to pull the empty trucks up the slope.

At Llanfoist the two systems met. The track up the hillside behind the white house is on the line of the old inclined plane. Trucks came down the slope and their contents were unloaded into the stone warehouse for transfer to boats on the canal.

This system was very efficient — although The Duke of Rutland, travelling the region in the early 19th century, recorded an accident when a waggon broke loose from its cable and hurtled down the hillside, landing in the branches of an ash tree. Today, however, the towpath of the canal is quiet, occupied by walkers and anglers instead of winded horses, and the old tramway forms a pleasant, broad track around the hillside for walking. Taking this route brings you right back to the beginning of the transport revolution.

From Llanfoist, the tramway track climbs up the mountain and passes through a tunnel to Blaenavon, now a Pit Mining Museum. The trucks on stone sleepers were pulled by horses.

sleepers and along the way lies an old tramway tunnel.

It was along this track that the trucks came to be lowered down the hill to Llanfoist. From here are the best views of the entire walk, down to Abergavenny with its old castle, right up the Usk Valley to the hills of mid Wales and across to the east where the A40 is a prominent feature, snaking away to Monmouth and the Wye Valley. There is one other fine view to be enjoyed: the Punchbowl **D**. This is a natural amphitheatre, where the slopes are heavily wooded with a little lake nestling in the bowl.

In the hollow of the Punchbowl lies a natural lake with an island in the middle.

LLANTHONY PRIORY

Early Christian sites in the Black Mountains

The peaceful Vale of Ewyas, where the walk takes place, is situated at the eastern edge of Brecon Beacons National Park. On the east bank of the River Honddu, which flows through the valley, lies an ancient site associated with St David, patron saint of Wales. It is here that the walk begins, continuing along an old pack-horse route that gives splendid views of the surrounding countryside.

In the 12th century, an impressive priory for Augustinian monks was founded on the ancient site. This was Llanthony Priory Ⓐ and it gave the Vale of Ewyas an alternative name — Llanthony Valley. The name of 'Llanthony' came from the Welsh 'Llandewi Nant Honddu', meaning 'the church of St David by the Honddu River'.

FACT FILE

- ✳ Black Mountains, Gwent, Brecon Beacons National Park

- 🚗 Outdoor Leisure Map 13, grid reference SO 288278

miles 0 1 2 3 4 5 6 7 8 9 10 miles
kms 0 1 2 3 4 5 6 7 8 9 10 11 12 13 14 15 kms

- ◕ Allow 3 hours

- ◼ Long but gradual ascent to reach the Hatterrall Ridge. Steep near Landor's house 'The Sharple'. Take care if there is a likelihood of mist, which may hamper route finding. Sensible footwear and waterproofs essential

- 🅿 At public car park adjoining Llanthony Priory

- 🍴 Refreshments available at the Abbey Hotel

- 🚾 Toilets in car park

▲ *From the Priory cloisters, the monks could watch the deer grazing on the mountains. (inset) The curlews' bubbling song echoes across the valley.*

Tradition claims that St David came to this valley in the 6th century and built a small mud and wattle hut, where he lived as a hermit in prayer and meditation for several years. He established many churches throughout Wales, and a monastery at St David's in Menevia (later Pembrokeshire, now Dyfed).

ROMANTIC SETTING

Romantically situated in the heart of the Black Mountains, the Priory is a memorable building. From the western door, the Priory church is 200 feet (60 metres) in length and, with the two aisles, it measures 50 feet (15 metres) in breadth. The massive square tower in the centre was originally 100 feet (30 metres) high, supported by bold, pointed arches opening on to the choir,

THE WALK

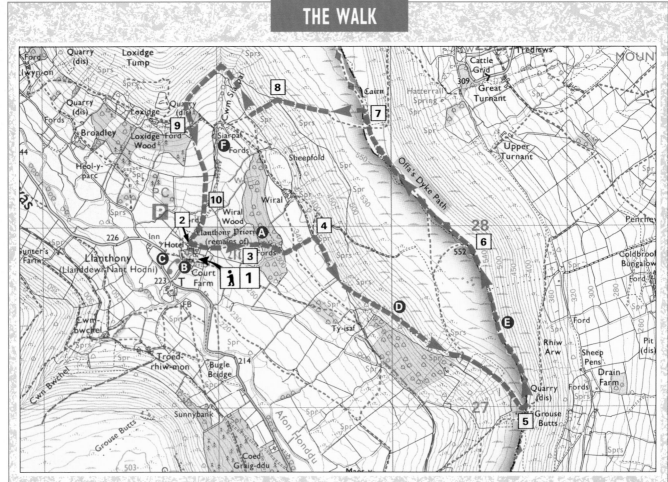

LLANTHONY-HATTERRALL RIDGE

The walk starts at the public car park adjoining Llanthony Priory Ⓐ.

1 From the car park, walk past the little church Ⓑ, cross the road and go over a stile beside a gate. Follow a stony track leading past the west front of the Priory. To the left can be seen a stone barn Ⓒ, once the gatehouse to the Priory.

2 On reaching a stile, turn right to walk beside a long stone wall adjoining the Priory ruins. At the end of the wall, go over a stile and head diagonally across to the top side of the field. (You may find this path temporarily diverted to follow the field edge.)

3 Go over a stile beside a gate and keep straight on,

following a broad track back up through a wood. Near the end of the wood go left over a stile and head straight up a field, keeping a fence on your right.

4 At the end of the field, go over a stile and turn right. (Ignore a waymark on the stile pointing left – it indicates the route of a shorter waymarked walk.) Follow a well-used path, which after about ¼ mile (400 metres) begins to ascend the hillside. It is known as the Rhiw Cwrw Ⓓ and the view opens out as you gain height. In due course the path levels out to follow a stone wall and then leads gently to the crest of the Hatterrall Ridge.

5 At the point where the track crosses the ridge, turn left to follow a path along the crest of the

ridge. This is the boundary between England and Wales and is also a section of the Offa's Dyke Long Distance path Ⓔ.

6 A triangulation point is reached and the track continues winding through the heather.

7 Turn left at the second of two cairns on the left of the track. Follow a faint path and head west down a slight slope. After about 200 yards (180 metres) you will reach a pointed cairn on the edge of the slope overlooking the Llanthony valley. From here a well-defined track leads down diagonally right.

8 On crossing the remains of a boundary wall, descend steeply to join a path leading past an oak tree. Soon you will see the remains of 'The Sharple' Ⓕ below, a house partly

constructed by the poet Walter Savage Landor. Head down to join a path beside the boundary fence. Further on it crosses two stream gullies in succession and then continues beside the boundary fence to reach a small wooden gate.

9 Go through the gate and keep straight on through the next field. Cross a cart track and continue straight on and down to a stile below in the trees. Pass through a little copse, go over another stile and bear right through the next field, heading towards the Priory. Cross a stile in a fence and walk through another field.

10 Go across an earthen bridge over a dingle and go over a stile beside a gate. The path then crosses a stream and joins a gravel track which leads you back to Llanthony Priory.

nave and transept. On the south side of the Priory is an archway giving access to a vaulted room with two floral bosses and carved capitals — this may have been the library.

ST DAVID'S CHURCH

By Llanthony Priory is a little church dedicated to St David **B** This Norman church was built on the site of the saint's cell. It is a very simple structure with an open-timbered roof. Of special interest is the fact that it is orientated for 1 March (St David's Day). The axis of the church points directly to that

Starting at Chepstow and finishing at Prestatyn in North Wales, this 168 mile (269 km) route follows for much of its length an earthwork built as a boundary in the 8th century by King Offa of Mercia. The path follows the Hatterrall Ridge, and there are wonderful views from it. To the right are the pretty patch-work fields of Herefordshire. And immediately below lies Cloddock Church and the long, straggling village of Longtown, whose name aptly describes it. In clear weather it is possible to see the Malvern Hills.

At the beginning of the 19th

Nature Walk

CAIRNS either signify a prehistoric burial site, or can be a path marker.

Powerful UPLAND STREAMS often contain boulders which have rolled down the stream bed, forced by the power of the water.

◄ *The little church by the Priory is dedicated to Wales' patron saint, St David. (below) Hatterrall Ridge, in the distance, is the boundary between Wales and England.*

part of the heavens where the sun rises on St David's Day.

Near the church is the old gate-house to the Priory. It has been converted into a barn and its great gateway walled up.

After leaving the Priory **C** and its environs, the walk continues along the Rhiw Cwrw. This is an ancient track which, like many in the Black Mountains, was estab-lished by farmers to provide an access route on to Hatterrall Ridge, where their sheep grazed. Rhiw Cwrw **D** translates as 'Beer Track' and it is believed to have been used by the monks for transporting casks of ale between Llanthony and Long-town in the next valley.

The path along the crest of the ridge marks the boundary between England and Wales and is part of Offa's Dyke Long Distance Path **E**

The Church by the Honddu River

Walter Savage Landor (1775–1864)

Llanthony Priory was founded in the 12th century. At that time the Vale of Ewyas belonged to the Lord of Ewyas and one of his retainers, William de Lacy, when hunting, came across the ruins of St David's cell. Overcome by the peace and sanctity of the valley he decided to remain there as a hermit.

After a few years he was joined by Ernisius, chaplain to Henry I, and together they built a church on the site of St David's hermitage. With the backing of Hugh de Lacy, the Marcher Lord of Hereford, they then founded a priory of the Augustine Order for Black Canons and 40 monks came to it from various parts of England.

In 1135, a Welsh uprising brought the Priory to a state of siege, so a year later the monks moved to Gloucester where a new priory was founded. One prior and four canons were left in the Black Mountains. It became a place of banishment where offending brothers were sent to suffer penance, and continued until the dissolution of the monasteries in 1536, when it was valued at £99.19s.

The Priory and its property were then granted to a royal servant, Richard Arnold, who later sold it to Auditor Harley, by which means it came into the hands of the Earls of Oxford. From them it passed to Colonel Mark Wood of Brecon. He converted the South Tower into a shooting box and built a house for his steward, which is now the Abbey Hotel. Colonel Wood sold the estate to the poet Walter Savage Landor in 1809 for £20,000.

Landor had grand ideas for restoring the Priory to its former glory and spent a vast sum of money on landscaping. He planted thousands of trees and even imported sheep from Spain.

Unfortunately he quarrelled with his neighbours and his tenants, who uprooted his saplings and refused to pay their rents. After frittering away his fortune, Landor left the valley in

The remains of the monumental tower built at the centre of Llanthony Priory.

1813 and vowed never to return. He died in his 90th year in Florence, having been forced to leave Britain due to acute financial problems. Today the Priory is established as an Ancient Monument and part of the building is a bar in the Abbey Hotel.

◄ The stable block is all that is left of 'The Sharple', Landor's unfinished house, now in ruins.

century, Llanthony Priory was bought by the poet Walter Savage Landor. Among the grandiose plans he had, one was to build himself a mansion in the woods overlooking the Priory. It was called 'The Sharple' ❻ and although the building was started, it was never completed. Today it lies in ruins.

The solitude and peacefulness of the valley encourages bird life, which is quite varied. In the early spring the ring ouzel and the wheatear arrive, the former to nest later in the year amongst the heather and the latter amongst the boulders and old walls. Peewit and green plover are frequently seen and meadow pipits abound. A few

▶ A few minutes walk from the Priory, one of many streams to be found in peaceful Llanthony Valley.

pairs of stonechats and whinchats may also be heard, and overhead you may observe a hovering kestrel or hear the croak of a passing raven.

THE 365 STEPS

◄ *The view over the Wye Valley is well worth the 365-step climb on a clear day. The thieving jackdaw (inset) has found an ideal place to hide his spoils. Penterry Church (below) hidden in the trees.*

described and praised by many authors of books on the Wye Valley and it used to be claimed that nine counties — before the new county boundaries were redrawn — could be seen from here. One writer observed: 'What a cathedral is among churches, the Wyndcliff is among prospects'. Below, the River Wye sweeps around the graceful Lancaut Peninsula and the wooded grounds of Piercefield Park, which contains Chepstow Racecourse. Further on, the Severn Estuary is spanned by the Severn Bridge.

IRON WORKINGS

A waymarked trail, the Wye Valley Walk **C**, follows the river valley from Chepstow to Hay-on-Wye — a distance of about 75 miles (120 km). Descriptive map packs of this route are usually available from local Tourist Information Centres. Here can be seen man-made depressions in the ground **D**, which are old iron workings, originally worked by the Romans. Set on the

---

A challenging walk up steps to a stone parapet with breathtaking views

---

The walk begins with a fairly steep climb up a flight of steps traditionally known here as 'The 365 Steps' **A**. They originally commenced from the rear of Moss Cottage, which was a thatched stone building that used to stand near this point. Here, tourists were able to buy refreshments and would then pay a small fee to walk through the garden and ascend the steps to the top of the Wyndcliff to admire the magnificent views. A certain Osmond Wyatt, the then Duke of Beaufort's steward, constructed the steps in 1828 and it is assumed that he probably built Moss Cottage as well. Restoration of the steps was carried out in 1972 by the Lower Wye Valley Preservation Society.

The Eagles' Nest **B** is a semicircular stone parapet on the very edge of the Wyndcliff. It is 700 feet (213 metres) above the Wye and was constructed as a viewpoint in the 19th century. The view has been

FACT FILE

✳ Lower Wye Valley, Gwent

▭ Pathfinder 1131 (ST 49/59), grid reference ST 527972

miles 0   1   2   3   4   5   6   7   8   9   10 miles
kms 0   1 2 3 4 5 6   7 8 9 10 11 12 13 14 15 kms

◷ Allow 3½ hours

▲ The walk ascends a series of steps leading up through a gap in the cliffs. They are fairly steep in places, but the views are very rewarding. Young children should be closely supervised on this ascent

P Small car park, signposted off the A466, in an old quarry just below the Wyndcliff on the left side of the A466, when travelling towards Tintern

THE WALK

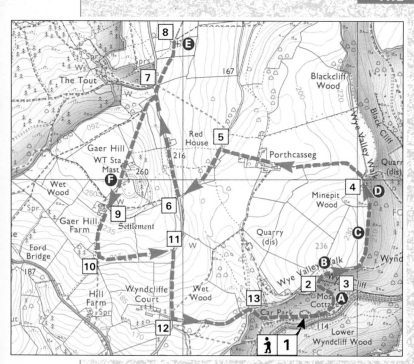

THE EAGLES' NEST – PENTERRY

The walk begins in the car park of the old quarry off the A466, 1 mile (1.6 km) north-east of St Arvans.

1 From the car park in the old quarry, follow a waymarked path leading around a rocky corner and then up through the trees to reach the start of a long series of stone steps, which are traditionally referred to as 'The 365 Steps' **A**. Continue upwards through the trees, passing boulders of moss-covered limestone, following a path safeguarded by rails and you quickly gain height. In due course you will reach an old ship's ladder bridging a gully and leading to a small platform where a good view may be enjoyed. Then continue up the final flight of steps, which are quite steep and bring you to the crest of the Wyndcliff.

2 Just past a seat, turn right and follow a path along the top of the cliff. Soon you will see a sign directing you down some steps, which lead to the Eagles' Nest viewpoint **B**.

3 After enjoying the expansive view, go back past the steps and follow a well-used track, which follows a section of the Wye Valley Walk **C**. It wanders through the woods and in due course passes some hollows in the ground **D**. Look out for a gate on the left, where two radio masts can be seen on the hill directly ahead.

4 Go through the gate and, keeping a hedge on your left, walk around the edge of a field. Then go through another gate and continue to join a lane leading past Porthcasseg Farm to reach a T-junction.

5 Turn left here and follow the lane to reach another T-junction.

6 Now turn right and follow a quiet country road through this peaceful and beautiful corner of Gwent.

7 By a footpath sign on the right, go through a gate and bear diagonally left to a stile in a hedge. On the other side go straight across the next field to reach Penterry Church **E**.

8 After exploring the church retrace your steps back to the road (at Stage 7). Turn left and shortly, just before some power lines, go up two steps and over a stile on the right. Head up through the field and bear slightly left to pass between a holly and a prominent oak following a distinct path towards the two radio masts on top of the hill. On the crest of the ridge, just in front of the masts, go through a gate. Walk across the next field and just past the masts go over a stile on the left to follow a tarmac drive, which leads across the summit plateau of the Gaer hillfort **F**.

9 Follow the drive down past Gaer Hill Farm and after about 150 yards (137 metres) go left past some trees to reach a stile.

10 Go over the stile and then immediately left through a gate. Continue through the next two fields, passing through two gates to join a tarmac road.

11 Turn right and follow the road downhill for a distance of about ¾ mile (1.2 km), to reach another road junction.

12 Turn left here and follow a quiet lane down to the Upper Wyndcliff Car Park. (This is an alternative starting point for the walk if you wish to avoid the steep ascent of 'The 365 Steps', because a path leads from here directly to the Eagles' Nest.)

13 From the back of the car park follow a path down through the trees back to the starting point.

slope of a hill, half hidden by trees, the isolated and picturesque little church at Penterry **E** stands on an ancient site, although the present building dates almost entirely from Victorian times. It was once a possession of the great abbey of Tintern and it is dedicated to St Mary.

The oval Iron Age hillfort of Gaer Hill **F** stands 800 feet (245 metres) above sea level and measures about 300 x 200 yards (278 x 180 metres). Traces of its outer embankment, with an entrance visible on the east side, can be seen. The inner defence and the outer western embankment have long since vanished. From this vantage point there are panoramic views of Wyndcliff, Tidenham Chase, the Wye Valley, the Severn Estuary and the Sugar Loaf, Skirrid Fawr and the Black Mountains.

▶ *The aptly named Eagles' Nest, high above the River Wye, is perched right on the very edge of the Wyndcliff.*

BOULDER AND BOULDER

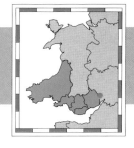

◄ *The Buck Stone was once a sacred Druid site. The pearl-bordered fritillary (above) was called the April fritillary until the calendar was put back 11 days in 1752 and it was not seen until May.*

A cross-border walk between Gwent and Gloucestershire

A Gloucestershire village on the edge of the Forest of Dean is the starting point of this pleasant walk. It also takes you into the county of Gwent and provides splendid views across the Wye Valley.

Staunton is a tiny village surrounded by Highmeadow Woods, owned by the Forestry Commission. Over 20 different species of trees can be identified and the woods support a wide variety of wildlife. The Forest of Dean was once a Royal Hunting Forest and fallow deer are the only reminder of the wild beasts, now hunted to extinction, that once provided sport for kings. There are two herds in Highmeadow Woods around the area of Staunton. They are extremely timid creatures but if they are approached upwind at dawn or dusk, you may catch a glimpse of them.

The main features to be visited on the walk are some large boulders of conglomerate rock which, over the years, have become local items of curiosity. The walk leads through mixed woodland on well-trodden and easy-to-follow paths. There are a couple of brief ascents involved but they are not too steep.

ROCKING STONE

The Buck Stone Ⓐ, situated at a point 915 feet (379 metres) above sea level on an escarpment of quartz conglomerate, is a large hunk of rock that at one time used to live up to its name and would rock if pushed in a certain direction. In 1885 a troupe of acrobats visiting Monmouth went up to Staunton on 10th June to visit the Buck Stone and managed to rock it so violently that it fell off its pedestal and shattered into pieces in the field below. There was a local outcry at this act of vandalism and it was subsequently repaired and replaced, at a cost of £500, but unfortunately its former equilibrium could not be restored.

Local belief has it that the Buck Stone was once a sacred Druid site and that a nearby hollowed stone was used for sacrifices. Also, anyone who walks around the stone three times as the sun rises may be granted a wish. The view from here is quite extensive, taking in the Wye Gorge and the Forest of Dean. In particular, the Newland Meander, which is one of the largest abandoned meander channels on the River Wye, can be seen.

Standing on a hilltop, Staunton church Ⓑ has a 14th-century central

---

FACT FILE

⚹ Staunton in Gloucestershire, on the A4136

🗺 Outdoor Leisure 14, grid reference SO 548126

miles 0 1 2 3 4 5 6 7 8 9 10 miles
kms 0 1 2 3 4 5 6 7 8 9 10 11 12 13 14 15 kms

◷ Allow 3 hours

▬ A relatively easy walk. There are a couple of brief ascents involved but they are not steep and the paths are well used and easy to follow

🅿 In the White Horse Inn car park, with the landlord's permission, or in a village side road such as Well Meadow Road, which is just south of the inn

🍴 The White Horse Inn, Staunton

THE WALK

THE BUCK STONE – THE SUCK STONE

The walk starts from Staunton village near the White Horse Inn. Be sure to ask permission if you leave your car in the pub car park. Otherwise park in Well Meadow Road, which is about 50 yards (45 metres) south of the inn.

➡ Follow the pavement past the White Horse Inn in a northerly direction to turn left up a lane. On reaching a gate across the road, go up a narrow path ascending the bank on the right and then on beside a stone wall. Follow the crest of the ridge for about ¼ mile (400 metres).

2 On reaching an underground reservoir go right through a gap in the wall to reach a trig point. Below a cluster of rocks is the large mass of the Buck Stone **Ⓐ**. After examining these curiosities and taking in the extensive view, return to the main track on the ridge and, after a few

paces, follow the track down to the left past the covered reservoir.

3 On reaching a tarmac lane turn left and follow it back towards Staunton village, which is now clearly in view, directly ahead.

4 At a road junction go right and then shortly left. At the next junction in the village go right and walk up the hill to reach Staunton church **Ⓑ**. After visiting the church follow the pavement along the side of the main road, back towards Staunton.

5 Cross the road with care and go up Well Meadow Road; bear right and join a gravel forest

track that leads on through the woods to later pass Redding's Lodge, a stone cottage picturesquely situated in a clearing.

6 On reaching a junction of tracks, take the first path on the left. Bear right at the next junction and shortly you will reach the top of the Near Hearkening Rock **Ⓒ**. Follow the path down to the right and pass below the overhanging rock. Near the end of it, follow a path to the right descending diagonally through the trees, to the Suck Stone **Ⓓ**.

7 Below the Suck Stone turn left up a broad forest track, which is followed for about ½ mile (800 metres).

8 Just after a rise and as the track descends, go left up a narrow waymarked path leading through the trees. On reaching a T-junction turn right and bear right at the next junction. On reaching the main road, turn left to follow the pavement back to the start.

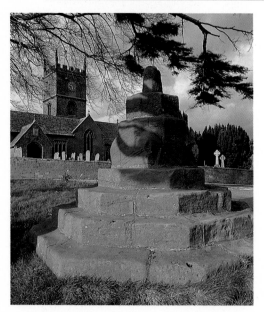

▲*The remains of the preaching cross in the churchyard stand in the shadow of Staunton's Early English-style church.*

tower and spire. Beside the road, in the churchyard, are the remnants of an impressive preaching cross. There are two fonts in the church. One dates from the 15th century and the oldest one has been carved from a Roman altar stone by a Norman mason. The 15th-century stone pulpit is reached by a winding staircase which once led to the rood loft.

NEAR HEARKENING ROCK

Further along you will reach the enormous overhanging rock called Near Hearkening Rock **Ⓒ**. It was once a favourite listening point used by the forest gamekeepers who would come here to listen for poachers who might be operating in the surrounding woods.

The Suck Stone **Ⓓ** is an enormous conglomerate boulder, said to be one of the largest boulders to be found in England and Wales.

▼*Gamekeepers once listened for poachers in the surrounding woods at Near Hearkening Rock.*

FOLLIES AND FORTS

A walk beside a Gothic castle and an Iron Age hillfort

This circular walk passes through the beautiful, unspoilt countryside of the Usk Valley. It includes a remarkable romantic folly — a Gothic-style castle built by a

FACT FILE

* Near Bettws Newydd in Gwent, off A40

* Pathfinder 1110 (SO 20/30), grid Reference SO 361084

| miles 0 | 1 | 2 | 3 | 4 | 5 | 6 | 7 | 8 | 9 | 10 miles |
| kms 0 | 1 | 2 | 3 | 4 | 5 | 6 | 7 8 | 9 10 | 11 12 13 14 15 | kms |

* Allow 3½ hours

* A pleasant walk with relatively gradual gradients and easy, well-used paths

* P In a National Trust car park situated a short distance from the river bank where seats are available for those who prefer to relax while the rest of the party enjoy the walk

* The Clytha Arms is ¼ mile (400 metres) north of the car park — turn right at the T-junction, it is up the hill on the left. Lunches and bar snacks

▲*The lush, green Usk Valley is an area of beautiful, rolling countryside. May is a particularly lovely month in this part of Wales when the woodlands are carpeted with bluebells (inset).*

broken-hearted landowner as a memorial to his departed wife — and an Iron Age hillfort. From this hill-top citadel, you descend into the valley to visit an exceptionally pretty little church and then you return along a waymarked path that forms part of the Usk Valley Walk.

CLYTHA CASTLE

Clytha Castle Ⓐ, the first point of interest on the walk, is perched on a hillside. You can see its ornate battlements through the trees. It was constructed in the Gothic style in 1790 by William Jones of Clytha House as a memorial to his wife,

◄*The walk begins at a kissing gate, where the path leads to the remarkable folly, Clytha Castle.*

THE WALK

FROM CLYTHA CASTLE THROUGH THE USK VALLEY

The walk starts from a National Trust car park situated beside the road from Clytha to Bettws Newydd about ½ mile (800 metres) south of A40.

1 On leaving the car park, turn left along the road and after a short distance go right through a kissing gate. Continue past a waymark post to reach a fence. Now follow a path to the left. You will now see Clytha Castle **A** which is directly ahead of you.

2 Bearing slightly left, walk across a field to reach a stile. Now cross the driveway to the castle and follow a narrow path through the trees to reach a stile at the end of the wood. Continue across the next field and then follow the fence to the left. Cross over a stile in the corner of the field; turn immediately right. Now follow the hedge to the corner of a field, turn left and carry on to reach another stile in the very top right corner of the field. From here continue via two more stiles until you reach the road.

3 Turn right along the road and follow it for about ¼ mile (400 metres). On reaching the junction, go straight on then, after about 200 yards (180 metres), go over a stile on the right. Walk across the next field and then go over a ladder stile on the right. You have now arrived at the prehistoric hillfort of Coed y Bwnydd **B**.

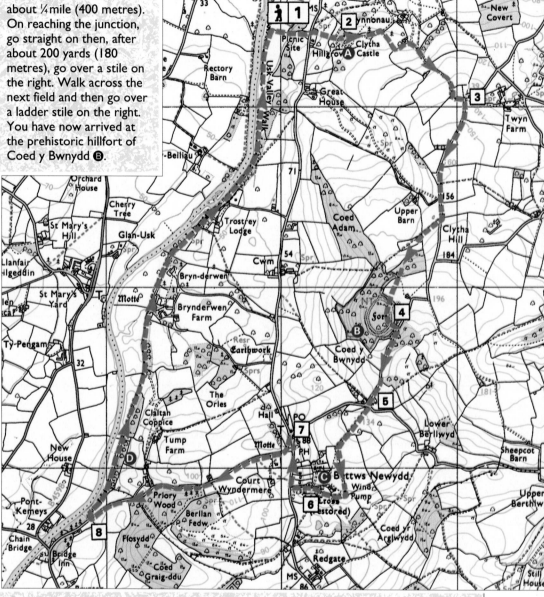

and a plaque on the side of the folly informs you that:

'This building was erected in the year 1790, by William Jones of Clytha House Esq., Fourth son of John Jones of Llanarth Court, Monmouthshire Esq., and Husband to Elizabeth the last surviving Child of Sir William Morgan of Tredegar, K.B. and Grand-daughter of the most noble William, Second Duke of Devonshire. It was undertaken for the purpose of relieving a Mind Sincerely afflicted, by the loss of a most excellent wife.'

The castle has been restored by the Landmark Trust and is available nowadays for rental as holiday accommodation.

AN IRON AGE HILLFORT

After walking through the fields, you reach the fortified hilltop of Coed y Bwnydd **B**. According to one local legend, it was once the site of a castle built by a giant named Clytha — but it is, in fact, the site of an Iron Age hillfort.

It is roughly oval in shape and covers an area of about 8 acres (3.2 hectares). A single rampart has been formed on the steep north and

north-west sides; however three trenches protect the other sides and a tumulus guards the entrance to the fort.

The name Coed y Bwnydd is variously translated as 'wood of the gentry' or 'wood of spearheads' and it would seem that it was occupied and strengthened by the Romans in the middle of the 1st century AD. It is now owned by the National Trust.

Archdeacon Coxe travelled here in 1798 and later described his visit in his book 'Coxe's Tours in Monmouthshire'. Recalling the fort, he said that: 'The western side over-

■➤ After exploring the hillfort, follow a track down to the left to reach a stile on the eastern side of the fort. Go down some steps and turn right along the road.

■➤ Turn left at the junction and after a short distance, go right over a stile. Follow the hedge on your left via three more stiles, and then take the path down and around to the right beside a long stone wall. At the end of the wall go over a stile and enter the churchyard of Bettws Newydd ◉.

■➤ Having explored the church, go out through the main gate and turn left along a lane. On reaching a junction, turn right and follow the road into Bettws Newydd village.

■➤ Just past the Black Bear Inn, turn left and follow a country road for about ¾ mile (1.2 km).

■➤ Go over a stile on the right waymarked 'Usk Valley Walk' ◉ and follow a path through a wood to reach another stile. Then continue through a field below the wood to pass through two gates and beneath Brynderwen Farm. The waymarked path continues close to the river for about 2 miles (3.2 km) and brings you back to your starting point.

◄*Clytha Castle is a truly romantic folly. It was built in 1790, as a memorial by a grieving widower.*

▶ *There has been a church here in Bettws Newydd since 1188 when Baldwin, Archbishop of Canterbury, visited the area.*

hangs the meandering Usk and commands a beautiful view of the northern parts of the county which will amply repay the traveller for the trouble of ascending the summit.' Today we are unable to enjoy the view that the Archdeacon saw because the trees have grown tall and dense. Nevertheless, you will be well rewarded if you come here in the bluebell season when the summit is richly carpeted in blue.

BETTWS NEWYDD CHURCH

After a short walk, you reach the churchyard of Bettws Newydd ◉. The first church on this site was founded in 1188 by Aeddan, who was the son of Gwaethfoed, Prince of Cardigan, and related by marriage to the King of Gwent. He also founded churches at nearby Bryngwyn and Clytha in honour of the visit of Baldwin, Archbishop of Canterbury. The Archbishop was on a tour of Wales at the time, bringing news of the Third Crusade.

Bettws Newydd Church was reconstructed between 1480 and 1520 and, in 1872, the interior was restored. Its greatest treasure is, without doubt, the carved screen and rood loft — the most complete example of its kind in Wales.

A UNIQUE SCREEN

It fills the whole space from the floor to the open roof, dividing the chancel from the nave. It is in perfect condition and represents a unique example of 15th-century craftsmanship, adorned with carvings of grapes, oak leaves and acorns and with a balustrade deeply cut with rich tracery.

The screen was probably constructed at the end of the 15th century to replace an earlier one and it thankfully survived the general destruction of church fittings that took place in the reign of Edward I. Access to the loft and gallery is via a door in the south wall, from which a staircase ascends, built in the thickness of the wall.

◄*The finely carved 15th-century screen and rood loft is a rare example of such craftsmanship in Wales.*

▲ *The ancient churchyard of Bettws Newydd has some equally venerable yew trees growing in it.*

On the west side of the church is an oak door, studded with hand-made iron nails, mounted on two heavy iron hinges. In the wall on either side are recesses for a slip-bar which could be placed in position to barricade the door from the inside — a reminder that churches often served as places of refuge in troubled times.

The ancient font is lead-lined with semi-circular carvings on the

▼ *The last stretch of the walk takes you along the waymarked Usk Valley Walk close to the river.*

Iron Age Defences

Hillforts were the most important defensive positions of the prehistoric age. They date from as early as 1500 BC up to the years immediately preceding the Roman Conquest and vary in size from 600 acres (240 hectares) to just 1 acre (0.4 hectare).

They were always strategically sited on top of steep slopes which made them easier to defend, as well as providing a good vantage point from which any approaching enemy could be seen in advance.

Simple hillforts were surrounded by a single bank and ditch, but the more complex ones often had multiple and overlapping ramparts to improve their defences. The gates — weak points in any defensive system — were often strengthened by guard chambers. The local tribe would herd the cattle inside the stockades, and the women and children would take refuge inside thatched wooden huts on the flat top of the fort. There were storage pits along rudimentary streets — so that the tribe would be well-equipped for a long siege.

Excavations have shown that the forts were sometimes abandoned for long periods of time and then, when a new enemy such as the Romans or the Saxons arrived, they were strengthened and brought back into use. Many of them were stormed by Roman legions and most were certainly abandoned after the Roman Conquest, when an era of peace prevailed until the Saxon invasions that started in 410 AD.

In Wales, hillforts are generally known as Gaers, like Gaer Fawr, near Newchurch in Gwent. There are about 200 hillforts in Wales altogether — and approximately 3,000 in Britain — of which an impressive number are in Gwent.

At Maiden Castle in Devon, there is a classic reconstruction of an Iron Age hillfort, protected by banks and ditches.

side of the bowl. It is probably older than the church itself. There are three fine yew trees in the church-yard and these are very ancient, too. Notice the one nearest to the porch which has a younger one growing inside the hollow trunk.

THE USK VALLEY

The Usk Valley Walk ❿ is a way-marked route starting from the Ship Inn at Old Caerleon, and you follow this as you return. It runs through the Vale of Usk to Abergavenny and then follows the towpath of the Brecon and Abergavenny Canal to Brecon — a route of some 50 miles (80km). For a map pack of the route, write to the Brecon Beacons National Park Office, 7 Glamorgan Street, Brecon, Powys LD3 7DP, enclosing a cheque or P.O. for £2.00.

A varied walk across country and along a towpath

The beginning of the walk takes you through the Pontypool Park Gates **A**. These were made about 140 years ago in the local ironworks and are a fine example of wrought-iron work. Pontypool claims to be the home of the South Wales iron industry, for there were forges here as far back as 1425.

CURIOUS GROTTO

Along the way, you will encounter the Pontypool Park Grotto **B**, a stone curiosity built by Lady Molly Mackworth in about 1830. It is decorated inside with shells of all shapes and sizes. Unfortunately, the building is now unsafe and not accessible to the public.

On a low mound **C** used to stand the Pontypool Folly, a tall, battlemented tower. It was built as a summer house by the Hanbury family in the 18th century. The tower was demolished in 1939 in case it might prove a useful navigational landmark for any enemy

▲ *The unspoilt beauty of the Brecon and Abergavenny Canal, which forms part of the route. Easily distinguished by the shape of its leaves, arrowhead (left) grows on the water's edge.*

FACT FILE

☀ Near Pontypool, off the A4042

▭ Pathfinder 1110, (SO 20/30) grid reference SO 290003

miles 0 1 2 3 4 5 6 7 8 9 10 miles
kms 0 1 2 3 4 5 6 7 8 9 10 11 12 13 14 15 kms

◔ Allow 4–4½ hours

▭ Only one moderate ascent. The Roman Road can be slippery after rain

P If you are unable to park near the Pontypool Park Gates, a good alternative is Fountain Road or at the Pontymoel Canal Basin

THE WALK

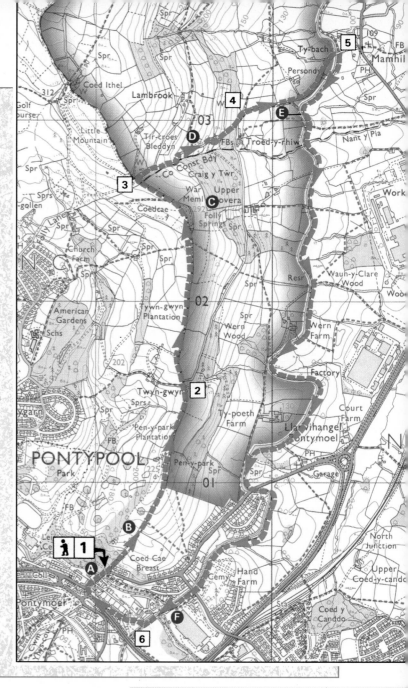

PONTYPOOL

The walk starts from the Pontypool Park Gates.

➡ From the ornamental gates Ⓐ go up a path by a footpath sign. It leads you beside a stone wall and ascends in a series of bends beneath overhanging trees. When the gradient relents and you emerge from the trees the views to the right start to open up. The wide track leads on through a gateway. Look out for a small metal ladder set in the wall on the left, from which a path leads up to the Pontypool Park Grotto Ⓑ just above. Then return to the lower track and continue along a wide track. Ignore a left turning.

➡ Keep straight on at the next junction and go over a stile beside a gate. The track leads on between hedges and follows the crest of the ridge. On the right, look out for a small RAF war memorial; just above it is a circular area of rocks that marks the site of

the old Pontypool Folly Ⓒ. Continue along the track to reach a gate.

➡ Turn right down a road and, shortly before reaching another gate, turn right down a path that leads down to yet another gate. From here an ancient stony track Ⓓ, showing evidence of cobbles in places, twists and turns down through a tunnel of trees. It is known locally as the Roman Road.

➡ On reaching a road, turn left and follow it down to a bridge spanning the Brecon and Abergavenny Canal Ⓔ.

➡ Turn right over a stile at the end of the bridge and follow the canal towpath to reach the Pontymoel Basin Ⓕ. Here you cross the canal on a stone bridge.

➡ Turn left along Fountain Road, and on reaching a road junction by a garage, cross over at the pedestrian crossing. Turn right along the pavement to return to the start.

aircraft. The views from this spot are very extensive.

Further on, you come to a stony track Ⓓ which runs downhill. This ancient route is reputed to be a Roman Road, but is more likely to be a medieval pack-horse route.

ALONG THE CANAL

The walk returns along a section of the Brecon and Abergavenny Canal Ⓔ, said to be one of the most beautiful waterways in Britain. It flows through the Brecon Beacons National Park and follows the Usk Valley from Brecon to Pontymoel. It is navigable throughout this distance, and organized boat trips start from both Brecon and Abergavenny.

The Pontymoel Basin Ⓕ used to be at the junction of the Monmouthshire

Canal and the Brecon and Abergavenny Canal, which officially ends here. In the Toll Cottage sat a toll clerk whose job was to gauge the boats and determine their load so that the appropriate toll could be charged.

Look out for water shrews, water voles, heron, dace, gudgeon, eel and carp on the canal. Insects of interest may include the waterboatman and dragonfly.

▲*View of the track which leads to the 'Roman Road'. High on a hill overlooking the countryside (left) stood the old Pontypool Folly.*

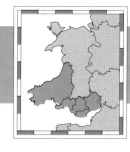

◄The calm, wooded Wye Valley can be glimpsed at the early stages of the walk. The flowers of the sycamore tree (below left) appear as drooping, mustard-yellow bunches.

is the start of a series of mills.

Once this was a busy industrial area. Wire was produced here in Tudor times, but by the early 18th century wire-making was ended and the water-powered mills found a new use, making paper. Tradition has it that the white paper for the old-style £5 note was made here.

There were five mills in all, and there is ample evidence of mill ponds and weirs, now transformed into attractive ornamental features. The best of the sites is Mill House **B** at the top of the hill, which includes extensive industrial buildings and its own mill pond.

TO THE COMMON

The road climbs steadily uphill beside the busy White Brook. Little cottages and grander stone houses now line the road all the way, clinging somewhat precariously to the steep hillside.

The route leaves the valley and turns off towards the woodland, beside an old wall of huge boulders

Through wooded hills flanking the River Wye

Mixed woodland blankets the hills rising above the Wye Valley and provides the setting for much of this walk, which also takes in fascinating historical remains ranging from a medieval well to Georgian paper mills.

The walk begins at the edge of Manor Wood on an old, roughly paved track, overhung by trees and bordered by an old, mossy drystone wall. As it clears the trees, the view begins to open out over the Wye Valley and its surroundings of wooded hills. It continues along a quiet lane between high hedges, liberally supplied with brambles.

WYE VALLEY WALK

At the large green, which has a scattering of houses, the route joins the long-distance Wye Valley Walk. It enters an area of dense woodland, dominated by sycamore. Through

the trees there are views of the River Wye itself down below.

Up ahead, there is the first view of the deep, densely wooded cleft of the Whitebrook Valley **A**. Looking slightly downhill to the right at the road, a house with ruined masonry walls adjoining it can be seen. This

FACT FILE

* Whitebrook, 4½ miles (7½ km) south-east of Monmouth

* Outdoor Leisure Map 14, grid reference SO 529058

  miles 0 1 2 3 4 5 6 7 8 9 10 miles
  kms 0 1 2 3 4 5 6 7 8 9 10 11 12 13 14 15 kms

* Allow 3 hours

* Good paths and country lanes, but hilly

* P Forestry Commission car park in Manor Wood

* T Infrequent bus service to Trelleck, from Chepstow or Monmouth

* Shop and inns at Trelleck

THE WALK

WHITEBROOK – TRELLECK

The walk begins at the Manor Wood car park.

1 ▶ Take the track back up towards the road, but turn left onto the footpath beside the fence just before rejoining the road.

2 ▶ At the road turn left.

3 ▶ At the large green, take the roadway to the right.

4 ▶ Where the lane ends, take the grassy track to the left. Then follow it around to the right and go steeply downhill.

5 ▶ At the roadway turn left onto path along Whitebrook Valley **A**.

6 ▶ Just past Mill House **B** turn left up a lane.

7 ▶ At the road junction, cross straight over to take the path beside the sign 'Trelleck Common and Beacon Hill'. Go straight on along the broad forest track and, as that swings away to the left, continue straight on along the narrower track and continue on this track, ignoring the forest tracks that cross it.

8 ▶ At the roadway, cross the stile and continue straight on along the footpath. In summer, if this is very overgrown, turn left onto the road and right at the junction.

9 ▶ At the road turn right. Cross a field with fence on right, then straight on along narrow path.

10 ▶ At the junction turn left into Trelleck, and continue to the end of the village street. Turn left on the road signposted Llandogo and continue past the Virtuous Well **C**.

11 ▶ Turn left by the Beacon Lodge.

12 ▶ Turn right at Beacon Farm onto a track leading to Beacon Hill Picnic Area, then immediately bear right again onto a narrow footpath that climbs steeply up through the woods. As it joins the wider path at the top of the hill continue straight on, ignoring forest tracks that cross.

13 ▶ At a tall pine tree ringed in red, go straight on along the path to the left of it and onto a surfaced road.

14 ▶ At the road junction, at the foot of the hill, by a telephone box, turn left and return to the car park.

▼ *The waters of the Virtuous Well are surrounded by a stone wall with seats for tired pilgrims.*

with large trees sprouting from its top. The path soon becomes an old packhorse route, roughly paved to give a grip on the steep sections. This is mixed woodland in which areas of oak stand next to plantations of young conifers.

Trelleck Common at the top of the hill is a more open area, with gorse and heather adding colour among the trees. The final part of this section of wooded walk is along an old track lined with beech trees.

Leaving the woods, views open out over farmland to the hills of South Wales. The way winds downhill towards Trelleck, dominated by its church tower and spire.

Translated, the name means 'village of stones' and relates to a trio of tall standing stones, probably erected in the Bronze Age, which are known as Harold's Stones.

VIRTUOUS WELL

The oddly-named Virtuous Well **C** was famous for its claimed cures for a variety of illnesses and was a place of pilgrimage. The springs are surrounded by a stone wall with seats for the weary pilgrims.

The final section is down a quiet lane, but the dark mass of conifers ahead promises a return to woodland. There is a last fine view before the path plunges off into the trees.

ON THE WYE GORGE

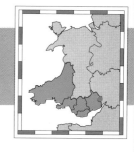

◀The broad reaches of the River Wye, a fine salmon river, pass between flowery banks below wooded slopes. The wild cherry (inset) can be found growing in the local woods and hedgerows.

A scattered village and old quarries above a lovely river valley

Penallt, where this walk begins, hugs the very lip of the famous Wye Gorge. The village's highly appropriate name derives from the Welsh words 'pen', meaning head or edge, and 'allt', which means cliff or hillside. The houses and farms are huddled around the village green, scattered on wooded promontories or standing beside swift shoots and waterfalls that tumble from the high plateau to the river far below.

WALLED CHURCHYARD

Penallt Old Church **A** clings to the steep hillside, its 13th-century tower anchoring it safely amid tumbling old gravestones in the tiny walled churchyard. Within the church, old memorials have survived the Victorian restorers, including one to a local who died at the notorious Jamaican pirate city, Port Royal, the home of Captain Morgan.

Near the lychgate, a gnarled, medieval chestnut tree marks the start of an ancient trackway down to the River Wye. In a few places, there are mossy wayside stones still recognizable as pack stones, where porters once rested their loads on the steep ascent from the river. At one point, a slabbed and walled pathway **B** joins the route, its stones worn smooth over the years by the passage of countless millstones from the plateau-top quarries to the waiting boats below.

The steep tracks emerge beside the Wye at the site of a former ferry; a rusting pulley on a wooden pole is the only reminder of this old river crossing. A little downstream, another old river crossing is still very much in evidence. The old bridge **C** once carried the Great Western Railway (GWR) across the Wye on its winding route between Monmouth and Chepstow. The line was closed by Dr Beeching in 1964, but the bridge, with its unusual underslung footway, remains an invaluable local route.

The bridge had a station either side; Penallt Halt this end and Redbrook the other. They were possibly the two stations closest to each other on the whole rail network.

FORMER RIVER PORT

The Wye here is one of Britain's premier salmon rivers; fishing rights can cost thousands of pounds a season. Anglers' huts dot the river bank here and there. Below one of them **D**, the jetty incorporates several old millstones; others can be seen on the far bank. The stones were shipped downriver from here to Chepstow and Bristol, and from there throughout the Empire. The Wye was once a busy waterway, with shallow-draughted trows built at many small, local yards engaged in busy coastal trade in the Bristol Channel.

The millstones were worked from a sandstone conglomerate rock known locally as Puddingstone, in quarries on the plateau or cut into the steep valleyside. Several of the valleyside quarries **E** are in woodland beside the route of the walk; a short detour through the thick undergrowth reveals a moss-covered stone leaning against a wall, and unfinished ones lying beneath

FACT FILE

✳ Penallt, 1½ miles (2.4km) south-east of Monmouth, off the B4293

▭ Outdoor Leisure Map 14, grid reference SO 522106

miles 0 1 2 3 4 5 6 7 8 9 10 miles
kms 0 1 2 3 4 5 6 7 8 9 10 11 12 13 14 15 kms

◔ Allow 4 hours

▬ Several ascents and descents, steep in places. Some paths may be muddy

▥ The Bush Inn in Penallt, and
🍴 The Boat Inn on the River Wye opposite Lower Redbrook

THE WALK

PENALLT – THE ARGOED

The walk begins at the Old Church Ⓐ in Penallt.

1 ▶ Walk downhill on the surfaced road. Immediately beyond the drive to Hillside Farm, go left down the walled pathway. Follow this, then the rough roadway, past a few cottages. Eventually you come to a minor road. Turn left, then shortly left again down a 'No Through Road', a continuation of the old millstone tradeway Ⓑ. Walk between several cottages to the riverside.

2 ▶ Turn right and follow the path to The Boat Inn. Pass beneath a railway bridge Ⓒ, and follow the path through the riverside meadows. A short distance beyond the anglers' hut Ⓓ, turn right at a waymark arrow and climb up to the old railway line. Climb the steep, concreted driveway opposite. At a gateway, turn left and climb the steep, wooden-stepped path beside a garden wall. From the wooden post at the top, a short detour to your left leads to the old quarries Ⓔ. From the post, walk up to a white gate and go left up the road about 300 yards (270m).

3 ▶ Just after a slight kink in the road, go through the gap-stile on your left, and across the pasture to a stile opposite. Once past a hollow filled with holly, aim for the top-right corner of the long field. Pass through the gate near here, and cut the field corner to the slab-stile beneath the coppiced hazel trees.

4 ▶ Beyond the stile, keep to the top of the rough pasture. Walk along the track at the far end, past an old barn and through the yard of a house, to a minor road. Bear right up this. After about 200 yards (180m), you reach a footpath sign. Turn right, and walk along the line of trees up through the field, looking for a stile in the top hedgerow. Turn right along the minor road and continue around the bend.

5 ▶ Just beyond a bungalow, climb the slab-stile on your right and head towards The Argoed Ⓕ. Go through a black kissing-gate into the estate grounds. Cross the minor driveway and walk behind the old chapel and outbuildings. Remain with the main drive away from the house. Follow the redwood trees as the drive bends away left. Cross the stile and walk to the road. Go right, then right again down Lone Lane. After just over 200 yards (180m), as the lane steepens, turn back left along an old cartway, and walk to the village green of Pen-twyn.

6 ▶ With The Bush pub to your right, walk along the green way, away from the green. At the bend marked by a fir tree, climb the slab-stile beside the gate, and walk along the hedgeline to a further stile. Go right along the road. At a triangular junction, bear right, signposted 'Penallt Old Church'.

7 ▶ Opposite the entrance to 'Sycamores' go left over a new stile, down through the woods. Go straight across a surfaced road to a stile at the foot of the field, near a cottage. Go half right, and up a wide old cart track, crossing several stiles. Continue beyond an isolated barn, keeping the hedge/fence on your left, and enter the woods at the far end of the field. At the road, turn left uphill to return to the Old Church.

the tangled ivy and brushwood near the mouth of one of the workings.

Once over the lip of the plateau, the walk levels out to an easy stroll along field paths and back lanes lined with wild flowers. One of these paths passes behind a large mansion called The Argoed Ⓕ. A past owner was Richard Potter, Chairman of the GWR. His daughter, Beatrice Webb, was one of the founders of the Fabian Society. Another member of this group of intellectual socialists, George Bernard Shaw, was a regular house guest. Among the features of the estate is a splendid avenue of trees, including some massive redwoods.

Soon you come to Pen-twyn, where the Bush Inn offers refreshment by the village green. You continue on lanes and paths, finally entering woodland and reaching the road back to Penallt and the start.

▶ *All that remains of the former hand-winched ferry across the River Wye is this rusting pulley on a pole.*

RUINS AND RENOVATIONS

▲ *Restored in the 1960s, by writer and film director Stephen Weeks, Penhow Castle is now open to the public. The snipe fly (inset) can be seen on plants in summer.*

Contrasting castles and an ancient church in a secluded valley

Hidden in a peaceful and secret valley in an unspoilt part of Lower Gwent are three jewels in the crown of Welsh heritage. Pen-coed Castle is a magnificent ruin, almost as spectacular in dereliction as it must have been in Tudor times; at nearby Penhow, Wales's oldest continually inhabited castle now relives something of its former glory; while St Bride's Church, embowered by venerable yews, bears mute witness to a vanished village.

This walk visits all three, but begins in the town of Magor, which looks out over the Caldicot Level to the sparkling blue expanse of the Bristol Channel. Near the start is the ruined Procurator's House. The procurator, a wealthy priest well-versed in law, presided here 600 years ago over a court that settled

local disputes, rates of pay and boundaries. He also collected rents and taxes on behalf of the Church of Rome. The grandeur of his house shows that he was well rewarded.

ANGELIC ARCADE

Behind the ruin is St Mary's Parish Church Ⓐ, founded in the 7th century by St Cadwalader. A new church, with a central tower and elaborate nave arcades adorned with 28 spirited angels, was built in the 13th century. The ivy-clad remains of a late medieval priory

▼ *The ruined house of Magor's 14th-century procurator, who grew rich as a revenue collector for the Vatican.*

MAGOR – PEN-COED CASTLE – PENHOW CASTLE

The walk begins from the car park next to the ruin of the Procurator's House, near The Square in Magor.

1 Enter the graveyard of St Mary's Parish Church **A**. Head into Magor Square past the war memorial **B** and turn left. Take the next right and continue to a T-junction. Turn left and follow this road to the next T-junction.

2 Turn left then immediately right along St Bride's Road. Continue for about ½ mile (800m), passing under the motorway. Turn left into a narrow lane and follow this for ¼ mile (400m).

3 Just before the motorway, turn right into a field through the left-hand gate of two. Cross two waymarked stiles, then go straight across the next field. Pass through the gap in the double hedge, then bear slightly left across the field to another stile. Cross it, and follow the hedge on your left. Bear left onto a track through the wood. On the other side, turn right to skirt the woodland, then left towards Pen-coed Castle **C**, keeping the wire fence to your left.

4 At the castle, turn right. Follow the track between buildings and a dovecote. Go through the gate, then cross a field to a stile in the far left-hand corner. Go over the stile and turn right. Cross two more fields and stiles, keeping the hedge to your right. In the third field go through the gate in the corner, then bear right across the corner of the next field. Go through the gate and head for a stile in a wire fence.

5 Cross the stile and turn left towards the farm. At the end of the barn, turn

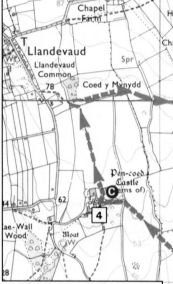

right. Go through the gate into the yard and turn left across the lane. Cross a step stile into Coed Wen woods. Keep on the woodland path to a T-junction and turn left. At the next T-junction, turn left again and follow the path uphill to a gate.

6 Go through into the field and turn right. Follow the field edge, then turn right down a farm track. Continue on through the gate then leave the track and head uphill. At the left-hand corner of the field, cross over the gate and turn left over another gate to visit Penhow Castle **D** and its church **E**.

7 Retrace your steps to the gate. Beyond it, turn left uphill. Continue over and down the hill, heading for the wire fence ahead and to your right. Turn right alongside the fence, then follow a track downhill

to Rock Lodge. Turn left through two gates and go over St Bride's Brook into St Bride's Lane.

8 Turn right. About 1 mile (1.6km) along the lane is St Bride's Church **F**. The medieval village **G** is through a gate on your right just before the Homestead on your left. Continue walking along the lane, passing Salisbury Farm **H**, to return to the car park in Magor.

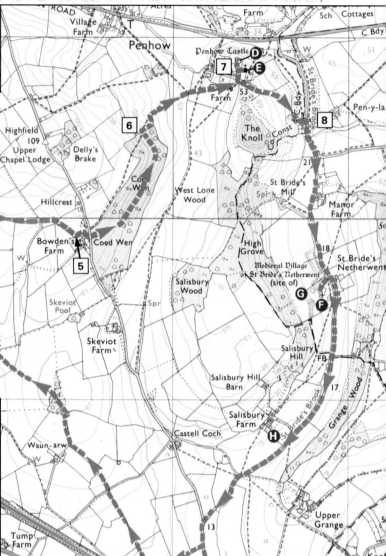

managed as a nature reserve, stretches out along the slopes of a dry limestone valley. Coppicing has been reintroduced to encourage indigenous ash, field maple, wild cherry and wych elm. Mighty oaks, limes and yews form a dense canopy over a woodland floor carpeted with enchanter's nightshade, bluebells, dog's mercury and wood anemones, as well as less common species such as Tintern spurge, wild daffodil, green hellebore, lesser periwinkle and bird's nest orchid — all sure indicators of ancient woodland.

The path winds uphill onto rich farmland. On warm summer days,

can be seen on the north-west side of the churchyard.

In the centre of Magor's pretty village square, enclosed by colour-washed buildings, is a huge war memorial **❸**. A handsome bronze medallion bears a portrait of Lord Rhondda, the Welsh mine owner and Liberal politician. During World War I, he was sent to the USA to negotiate the supply of munitions.

His success there earned him a peerage. On his death, in 1918, his daughter, Margaret Haig Thomas, who had been arrested for her suffragette activities, endeavoured to take her seat in the House of Lords as Viscountess Rhondda. She was only prevented from doing so after protracted legal proceedings.

HILL FORT AND CASTLE

As you cross an open field, Wilcrick Hill Iron Age fort rises beyond the M4 motorway to your left. Away to your right is Upper Grange Farm, which was once owned by the monks of Tintern Abbey.

Pen-coed Castle **❸** was once the stronghold of a Norman knight, Sir Richard de la More, though the majority of the building seen today dates from the reign of Henry VIII. In the early 1900s, it was part of the vast Herrick Estates of Leicester. Sophie Perry-Herrick, the Lady of the Manor, was a staunch teetotaller. She closed many of the pubs in Magor, including the Red House, the Half Moon, the Bell Inn and the Rock & Fountain. Following her

▶ *Empty, decaying and atmospheric, Pen-coed Castle is 13th-century in origin. Most of what is seen today is Tudor.*

▲*The route offers several views of Wilcrick Hill, site of an Iron Age fort, which rises to the south of the M4. The path continues across farmland (right) towards Pen-coed Castle.*

death in 1915, the castle became the property of Lord Rhondda, who was responsible for the modern extensions completed in 1920.

Today, Pen-coed is abandoned, not yet beyond reprieve, but quietly crumbling with each passing year. Himalayan balsam, red campion and wall pennywort colonize fissures in the paved courtyard, and jackdaws tumble in exuberant aerobatics between the decaying battlements of its once-mighty towers. The broken outlines of the castle and its ruined Tudor dovecote are an evocative sight.

Coed Wen, a semi-natural wood

ripening ears of wheat whisper in the breeze and a swaying field full of pale blue flax makes a truly unforgettable sight.

Penhow Castle **❹** (see box on page 40) and its church **❺** stand on the brow of a hill. The church was founded by the Normans, and rebuilt in 1914, though the tower still bears its distinctive arrow loops,

Penhow Castle

In the early 12th century most of Wales was controlled by local princes. The town of Chepstow was a rare Norman stronghold, defended by a surrounding ring of knights' castles. In 1129, Henry I entitled one of these knights, Roger de St Maur, to seize Penhow from its native prince as a reward for his help in suppressing the Welsh.

The St Maur (or Seymour) line prospered, and they became one of the most noble families in the land,

▲ *The woodland on the slope, Coed Wen, is a remnant of ancient forest.*

making their home at Penhow for around 400 years.

In the early 18th century, the castle had declined into a rather grandiose farmhouse owned by absentee landlords. Its fortunes were to fall further. By 1966, it was virtually derelict; the impressive spiral staircase, magnificent Lower Hall and Norman tower were little more than filth-encrusted chicken runs, granaries and apple stores.

In that year, writer and film director Stephen Weeks bought Penhow and set about gradually restoring it. The carpentry and masonry skills of past centuries were employed in a painstaking attempt to recreate the castle's authentic original atmosphere.

Today it portrays a cross-section of its past history, from the 15th-century Great Hall, with its elegant gallery from which minstrels serenaded the banqueters below, to a Victorian house-keeper's room, cluttered with domestic bygones.

As you wander through its labyrinth of rooms and corridors, you can almost hear the amiable crackle of logs, the hospitable sizzle of the mulling poker warming the wine and the heavy splash of meat bones, cast from the open window into the moat below.

The castle's 17th-century dining room is a tribute to the vision of the new owner who invested time and money in re-creating it.

Mayor of London into a horse.

The graveyard is all a country churchyard should be. Its timeworn yews once furnished longbows for the archers of the South Welsh Borderers. These marksmen fought in English armies against the French at Crécy, Poitiers and Agincourt, and also against the Scots.

LOST VILLAGE

A few grassy tumps in an adjacent field are all that remain of the once prosperous medieval village of St Bride's Netherwent **G**. The distinct mounds of houses congregate along a central hollow that marks the sunken village street. Nobody knows for certain how the community was wiped out, though it may have happened as early as the mid-14th century, when the Black Death swept through Europe.

Further on down the lane, on the way back to Magor, you pass Salisbury Farm **H**, a 17th-century building away to your right.

an effective rear-guard defence if the castle was under attack.

An inscribed tombstone in the porch commemorates one Elizabeth Tamplin, who died in 1783 at the remarkable age of 111. Inside, an unusual stone chancel screen was re-cut earlier this century. The columns on the south aisle still bear the marks of 18th-century box pews, whose high sides helped keep out the worst of the draughts.

BRIGID'S BELL

Down a quiet lane, at the heart of St Bride's Valley, is a lonely parish church **F**, built in the 1800s, but with a history dating back to the early 10th century. The inscribed angelus bell is dedicated to St Brigid. The many miracles of this Irish saint include changing stones into honey, ashes into butter and the Lord

▼ *Penhow Church was established by the Normans — note the tower — but underwent major restoration in 1914.*

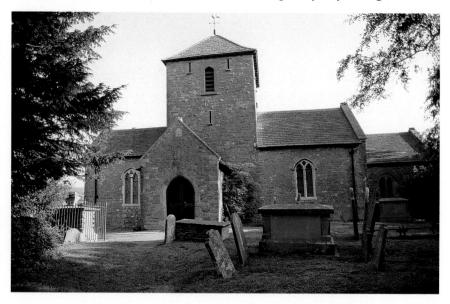

FACT FILE

* Skenfrith, 6 miles (9.6km) north-west of Monmouth, on the B4521

* Pathfinders 1064 (SO 42/52) and 1087 (SO 41/51), grid reference SO 457202

miles 0 1 2 3 4 5 6 7 8 9 10 miles
kms 0 1 2 3 4 5 6 7 8 9 10 11 12 13 14 15 kms

* Allow 4 hours

* One steep climb. Some fields blocked by crops. The path through Daren Wood may be very overgrown in summer — take a clearing stick.

* P Free parking by the castle at the start

* The Bell Inn in Skenfrith

Discover the architectural heritage of the Monnow Valley

For much of its length, the River Monnow forms the natural boundary of Wales. Many centuries of conflict between the Welsh and a succession of invaders — Romans, Saxons and, in particular, Normans (see box on page 44) — has left a rich heritage in this now peaceful borderland area. This walk explores a landscape of woods, hills and streams that has changed very little since the days of Llywelyn the Great and Owain Glyndwr.

ANCIENT VILLAGE

The valley contains some of the oldest villages in Britain. Among them is Skenfrith, which guards one of the rare gaps in the deeply incised Monnow Valley. A few cottages and houses line one side of the green, while the village's

▲Skenfrith, in the Monnow Valley, is dominated by its impressive castle. The American mink (left) is established by the river. The tower of St Bridget's Church (below) is topped by a dovecote.

THE WALK

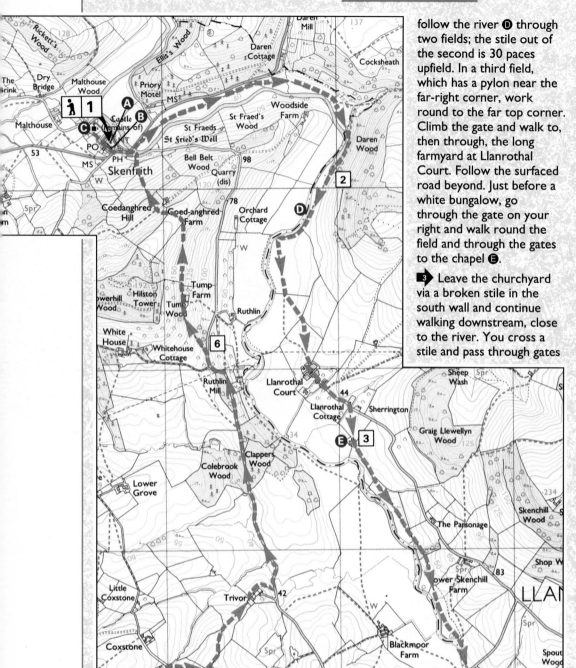

follow the river **D** through two fields; the stile out of the second is 30 paces upfield. In a third field, which has a pylon near the far-right corner, work round to the far top corner. Climb the gate and walk to, then through, the long farmyard at Llanrothal Court. Follow the surfaced road beyond. Just before a white bungalow, go through the gate on your right and walk round the field and through the gates to the chapel **E**.

3 Leave the churchyard via a broken stile in the south wall and continue walking downstream, close to the river. You cross a stile and pass through gates and down the drive. Within ten paces, a waymark arrow points left to a stile in the hedge. Cross, turn right and go over the footbridge in the bottom corner of the field. Keep the hedge to your right to the first ash tree, then angle slightly left up the field. Walk to the old barn in the next field. Ignore the stile just beyond the barn, but turn left up the long field to a stile near a pylon. Climb this and turn right to St Maughan's Church **G**.

5 Turn right from the churchyard and walk down the narrow lane. Just before the stream, go right at the footpath sign and head for the diagonally opposite corner of the field. Cross two stiles, then keep the hedge to your left for 100 yards (90m). Climb the stile and bear right, aiming for the left of the farm as it comes into view. Climb the gate, then enter the rough pasture on your left. Walk behind the barn and down to the bottom-right corner (or follow a footpath diversion). Turn left along the minor road, and follow it for a mile (1.6km).

6 Turn left up the drive to Tump Farm. Pass immediately left of the house and climb the stile/gate in the far right corner of the paddock. Angle slightly left up this steep field to meet the fence along the top about 20 yards (18m) right of the line of electricity poles. Climb the stile and bear half-left across the ridge top, to cross a stile in the fence. Near the bottom-right of the field, cross the stile. Continue down through rough pastures to the lane beside the white-painted Bell Inn.

SKENFRITH – ST MAUGHANS

*The walk starts on the green by Skenfrith Castle **A** and Castle Mill **B**.*

1 Walk up the road, with the green on your right, to visit the church **C**. Return to cross the bridge near the Bell Inn. Turn right on a riverside path signposted to Broad Oak Road.

2 When you emerge from the Daren Wood, to reach Tregate Bridge **F**. Cross this and follow the narrow road to St Maughan's Green.

4 At the junction, bear left. After a few paces, go right across the cattle grid

most obvious feature, the castle **Ⓐ**, dominates the other. The green itself covers part of the filled-in moat.

The castle dates from around 1200; the curtain walls enclose an unusual circular keep built on a distinct mound, which was possibly the site of an earlier wooden castle. It was constructed for Hubert de Burgh, a Duke of Kent who was a favourite of King John, and it was only in use for about 200 years.

WORKING MILL

The Monnow acted as a natural moat on one side of the castle. Once peace was established in the valley, a large weir was built to broach the river and supply water to Castle Mill **Ⓑ**, which was built in the filled-in moat. The mill is still busy today. Its great water-wheel (visible from near the war memorial) works hoists, lifts and grindstones that produce flour and animal feedstuffs. It is not open to the public.

The village's glory is the beautiful

▶ The route follows a tranquil stretch of the River Monnow, whose tree-shaded banks are a delight in summer.

little St Bridget's Church **Ⓒ**, which dates from around the same time as the castle. The squat tower is topped by a dovecote, while the spacious, stone-flagged interior houses a number of delights. These include wall paintings, a minstrels' box, the splendid family pew and relief tomb of the Morgan family (one-time lords of the manor), and a medieval embroidered cope (cloak), which was used as an altar cloth before its true worth was realized.

The route sets off downstream, darting in and out of woodland and thick undergrowth. The woods are home to a wide variety of birds of prey, including a surprisingly large number of buzzards.

MINK AND OTTERS

The Monnow is one of Britain's cleanest rivers. A quiet, isolated stretch **Ⓓ** supports several otter holts, though you are far more likely to see a semi-webbed pawprint in riverside silt than the animal itself.

This timid creature has slowly built up its numbers since the 1960s, when an extremely active pack of otter hounds hunted virtually the whole length of the river. Mink are now well established in the area, much to the chagrin of river keepers and fishermen, and keep a higher profile than the surviving otters.

Further along is the Chapel of St John the Baptist **Ⓔ**, virtually all that remains of an abandoned medieval

village. It succumbed not to the Black Death, but to a climatic aberration that led to a series of crop failures around 1400.

The chapel dates from the early 13th century, and is now in the care of the Redundant Churches Fund. Half of it is simply, almost puritanically furnished with old, movable wooden pews or settles, a carved pulpit and an ancient altar. There is no access to the other half, which is

▲ The Chapel of St John the Baptist was at the centre of a medieval village, but now stands in splendid isolation — the village was abandoned when freak climatic conditions led to several years of crop failure. The route leads across golden fields (right), where an old barn makes a very useful landmark.

▶The primitive simplicity of St Maughan's Church, in the hamlet of the same name, is enhanced by its setting.

visible through small windows on the south side and is totally unrestored. This area was a Catholic stronghold during the years of persecution. A local priest, John Kemble, was beheaded at Hereford in 1689.

Another peaceful stretch of river, its sandy banks home to kingfishers and colonies of sand martins, leads to the narrow, old Tregate Bridge ❻, built on an ancient routeway at the site of a ford. Below the bridge, a broken old weir can prove a good vantage point for watching salmon leap during their October run.

Nearby, a substantial motte and bailey, the mound of which is easily

▲Skenfrith Castle saw little action, and was abandoned by the middle of the 16th century. It now lies in ruins.

seen from beside the bridge, guarded the ford and offered protection for members of a nunnery and a priory that once stood in the woods in the folded hills beyond the castle.

You climb gently out of the valley, along lanes and pathways rich in wild flowers, to the 13th-century St Maughan's Church ❼, dedicated to one of the seemingly endless supply of Celtic saints. The massive timber pillars holding up the barrel-vaulted roof are nearly 600 years old, and replace the original stone ones destroyed when Owain Glyndwr laid waste to the church.

The return route from the church back into Skenfrith is a pleasant, gentle stroll through open fields, lanes and woodland.

The Welsh Marches & Marcher Castles

Following the Battle of Hastings, William the Conqueror moved fast to secure his new realm. The Welsh proved an immediate thorn in his side, so William appointed his three most trusted lieutenants to secure and control the troublesome English/Welsh border — The Marches. These Marcher Earls were virtually kings in their own realms, which were centred on Chester, Shrewsbury and Hereford.

The most visible signs of their presence are the castles constructed between the Conquest in 1066 and 1400. There are more castles in this area than anywhere else in Britain. Earl FitzOsbern and his successors in the southern Marches, Gwent and Herefordshire, built most of all.

Some, like Chepstow, Britain's first stone-built castle, were great fortresses, intended to impress on the Welsh (and, to an extent, the lower echelons of the Norman nobility) the invincibility and superiority of these royal favourites. Most, however, were of the tried and tested motte and bailey design. Their main function was largely symbolic, proclaiming the Norman presence to the local population.

Only very rarely was stone used in motte and bailey castles. The current monuments to yesterday's border wars are the earth mounds, nowadays often tree-covered, that are part of the landscape in even the tiniest hamlets in this area. An excellent example can be seen near Tregate Bridge on this walk.

The Monnow Valley was an enduring problem for the Normans and their successors, and three substantial stone castles were developed to control this natural routeway between England and Wales. Granted personally by the King to a succession of owners, the trilateral Castles (Skenfrith, White and Grosmont) played significant roles in the continuing campaigns against the Welsh Princes. These lasted well into the 15th century.

After this, the castles were largely devoted to local administration rather than to strategic uses. By this time, too, the power and influence of the Marcher Earls had waned, to be replaced by that of the abbots of large abbeys, the remains of which are also a prominent feature of the Welsh Marches.

The remains of a motte and bailey castle, just off the route near Tregate Bridge.

A short, easy walk on the edge of St Gwynno's Forest

The route around the edge of St Gwynno's Forest takes you through pleasant and varied scenery, with extensive views over farmland, the Clydach Valley and the forest itself. The walk leads you eventually to the tiny hamlet of Llanwonno, which is situated on Cefn Gwyngul at an altitude of 1,100 feet (335 metres). In the graveyard of Llanwonno Church you will find a gravestone that tells the story of a remarkable local athlete who became a legend in his own lifetime.

After walking through farmland, the route takes you into Llanwonno Forest **A**. This is a comparatively recent forest planted by the Forestry Commission, and in the heart of these new woodlands lies the secluded hamlet of Llanwonno.

TIME STANDS STILL

The small hotel, Brynffynnon Hotel **B**, is named after a nearby spring (ffynnon is Welsh for spring), which was once known as St Gwynno's Well. It is advisable to arrive here during opening hours at lunchtime in order to get the keys to Llanwonno Church **C**, since this is normally locked.

FACT FILE

- ✳ Ynysybwl, 3 miles (5 km) north of Pontypridd, Mid Glamorgan
- ▭ Pathfinder 1129 (ST 09/19), grid reference ST 051951

miles 0 1 2 3 4 5 6 7 8 9 10 miles
kms 0 1 2 3 4 5 6 7 8 9 10 11 12 13 14 15 kms

- ◑ Allow 3 hours
- ▬ An easy walk. No very steep ascents involved and the route follows lanes and forest tracks
- P On the northern outskirts of Ynysybwl at the junction of Mynachdy Road and Heol-y-Mynach, just above an old school is a wide area of road near a bus shelter
- 🍴 Shops in Ynysybwl. Brynffynnon Hotel along the walk

◀ Guto's headstone tells of his victory in a race against one of his major rivals.

A church has stood on this site for over 14 centuries and this one serves the extensive parish of Llanwonno — a daughter church is situated in the village of Ynysybwl about 3 miles (4.8 km) away. Llanwonno Church consists of a chancel, nave, south porch and a

▲ The hamlet of Llanwonno is dominated by the tiny church and its peaceful graveyard. Listen carefully for the song of the thrush (inset).

western turret with two bells.

The interior of the tiny church is well worth a visit. Of interest inside are two old fonts. In the south wall of the nave is a fragment of an ancient cross, which is probably pre-Norman. A small statuette of St Gwynno, the patron saint, can be seen above the entrance to the south porch. The Llanwonno churchyard

▲ Some parts of the tiny church at Llanwonno are thought to be pre-Norman.

THE WALK

YNYSYBWL – LLANWONNO

The walk begins at the parking spot at the junction of Mynachdy Road and Heol-y-Mynach just north of the village of Ynysybwl.

1 From the parking spot, go up Mynachdy Road and, when it levels out, turn left over an old stone bridge to follow a lane past a farm. Ignore the first footpath sign on the bridge, pointing to the right.

2 At the top of the hill go through a gate on the right by a footpath sign and follow a gravel track beside a fence. After about 100 yards (90 metres) leave the track and bear diagonally left across the field, aiming for an outcrop of rocks. Go through a gate between a fence and the end of a stone wall. Maintain height and keep straight on across the field to reach a stile in a fence by a footpath sign.

3 Go over the stile and turn left along a broad forest track leading pleasantly through a conifer plantation **A**. About 50 yards (45 metres) before a junction with a forest road, turn left to follow a path leading down through the trees. On meeting the forest

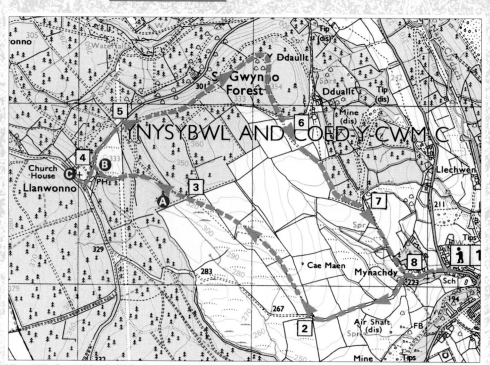

road, go straight across and up through the trees for 50 yards (45 metres) to reach a very dilapidated stile in a fence. Ignore the gate in the corner. Cross the stile and turn left, then right to follow a path beside the fence which leads to a road.

4 Turn left along the road and go past the Brynffynnon Hotel **B** to reach Llanwonno Church **C** and churchyard, which you will see on the right. After visiting the church

return along the road, passing the hotel. Go around the corner and continue along the road for 500 yards (450 metres) to reach a picnic area on the right.

5 Cross the car park and turn left to follow a track ascending through the trees and shortly join a forest road. Keep straight on and bear left at the next junction, enjoying occasional views through the trees across the valley to the hills on the other side. The track drops down and then starts

ascending again.

6 On emerging from the wood, continue over a cattle grid and then on to another cattle grid to follow the cart track down through the trees.

7 At a U-bend, follow the track round and shortly go through a series of three gates and past Mynachdy Farm.

8 On reaching a junction by the old stone bridge, you rejoin the outward route. Turn left here to the starting point.

▲ *From the forest there are views across the rolling hills to the Cynon Valley.*

is very large, covering an area of some 3-4 acres (1.2-1.6 hectares).

To the right of the south porch is Guto's Grave — the grave of Griffith Morgan of Nyth Bran Farm, which is in Llanwonno Parish. He was born in 1700 and won local fame as a runner. It was said that he could race a horse and he is reputed to have run 12 miles (15.6 km) in 53 minutes. Local people used to claim that Guto's mother would some-times send him to Aberdare on an errand and he would run there and back before the kettle had boiled!

He won many races, but one day, at the age of 37, after he had just successfully finished a race, a man slapped him on the back. Guto's heart stopped and he collapsed and died. However, his legend lives on in Llanwonno and his gravestone, recounting his prowess as an athlete and inscribed in Welsh (there is a translation), is always well tended.

Leaving Llanwonno, the route continues through the forest, giving some marvellous views of the Clydach Valley and, on a clear day, the Cynon Valley beyond.

GARTH HILL

The rounded eminence of Garth Hill **B** can be seen from far away and its distinctive summit is made even more prominent by the three prehistoric cairns that crown it. The summit mound was used at one time as a beacon site. A beacon lit here would be answered by others lit on Penarth Head and Cefn Onn, near Cardiff, to warn people of impending danger at a time when Britain was under threat of invasion.

◀*In the Bronze Age, people used to bury their dead in hill-top mounds, such as Garth Hill. The gudgeon (below) was historically considered a delicacy, in spite of its scant flesh.*

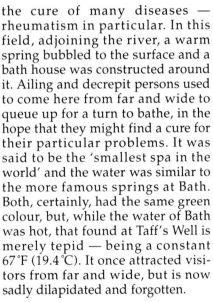

An energetic walk up a hill overlooking the Taff Gorge

Cwm Taf, or Taff Vale, was once an industrial area, where the presence of iron ore and coal led to the establishment of iron furnaces beside the River Taff in the 16th century. Brick making and stone quarrying were also at one time undertaken in this area.

Today, the scene is more peaceful and this walk leads through woods and farmland and along a spectacular ridge to provide extensive views of the surrounding countryside.

Taff's Well **A** was once famous for the cure of many diseases — rheumatism in particular. In this field, adjoining the river, a warm spring bubbled to the surface and a bath house was constructed around it. Ailing and decrepit persons used to come here from far and wide to queue up for a turn to bathe, in the hope that they might find a cure for their particular problems. It was said to be the 'smallest spa in the world' and the water was similar to the more famous springs at Bath. Both, certainly, had the same green colour, but, while the water of Bath was hot, that found at Taff's Well is merely tepid — being a constant 67°F (19.4°C). It once attracted visitors from far and wide, but is now sadly dilapidated and forgotten.

◀*The River Taff meanders along through Taff Vale. Sourced high in the Brecon Beacons, it carries some 6½ million gallons (30 million litres) of water every day down through Cardiff and into the Bristol Channel.*

FACT FILE

⚹ Taff's Well, Mid Glamorgan, off A470, 6 miles (9.5 km) north of Cardiff

▣ Pathfinder 1148 (ST 08/18), grid reference ST 119837

miles 0 1 2 3 4 5 6 7 8 9 10 miles
kms 0 1 2 3 4 5 6 7 8 9 10 11 12 13 14 15 kms

◔ Allow 3½ hours

◼ A steady climb to reach the summit of Garth Hill. Keep children back from the steep ground at point **C** where one overlooks the Taff Gorge.

🅿 Near the Taff's Well Inn in an adjoining road. Turn off by a bus shelter and the Fynnon Taf County Primary School

🏠 Taff's Well Inn

THE WALK

TAFF'S WELL – GARTH HILL

The walk starts from the Taff's Well Inn Park in the road to the right of the inn and near the Fynnon Taf County Primary School.

of the bridge you pass through a mini-subway. Turn left and follow a tarmac path that zig-zags up the hillside.

2 On reaching a road, turn right and then left by

continue, to gradually ascend the hillside.

3 On passing through two gates, carry on through the farmyard of Lan Farm, now enjoying more open views. Turn left at a road junction, then left again and shortly left yet again. Follow a lane which bears left at the next junction to then follow a

way. The summit is marked by a trig point on the top of a prehistoric burial mound.

5 Make your way back along the crest of the ridge, now following a section of a long distance walk, known as the 'Ridgeway Walk' (Ffordd-y-Bryniau). The track passes two more prehistoric mounds and then snakes around to a fine vantage point which gives you a bird's eye view of the Taff Gorge **C**. Follow the well trodden path down, and it shortly takes a diagonal line to the right, across to a road.

6 Turn left along the road and after about ½ mile (800 metres) go through a kissing gate on the right. Head down to another one on the edge of a wood and follow a pleasant path down through the trees. Ignore all left and right turnings and in due course you will reach a road.

7 Turn left here and after about 150 yards (135 metres) go right by a footpath sign to follow a path through a wood. Then turn left along a lane and shortly bear right along a gravel path, which follows the bank of the Taff and leads you back to the bridge crossed on your outward route. Retrace your steps from here back to the start of the walk.

1 To see the site of the famous Taff's Well **A**, go to the left of the inn and look across towards the river. You will observe a bricked-up, semi-circular construction, set in the side of the river bank. Go down the lane beside the primary school and bear right to reach a footbridge spanning the River Taff. At the end

the Gwaelod-y-Garth Inn. Follow this lane uphill, to keep straight on at the crossroads and then go right at a bend in the road. Now follow a path between a hedge and a wall. Go through a gate and

stony track leading up to the long-abandoned ruins of Garth Farm.

4 From here the broad, rutted track takes you straight up to the summit of Garth Hill **B**, with the view behind you unfolding all the

---

The Taff Gorge **C** has been created by the waters of the River Taff cutting their way through a ridge of hard rock, leaving almost vertical cliffs from which stone has been quarried. For centuries this valley was a vital route of communication and at one time two roads, two railways and a canal ran through it.

On the other side of the valley, looking in the direction of Cardiff, can be seen the towers of Castell

Coch — Red Castle. This is a sham castle built by the Third Marquis of Bute in 1875, in a style similar to that of a Rhône château. It does, however, stand on the site of a Norman fortress, built between 1260 and 1300 by one Gilbert de Clare to guard the Taff Gorge.

▶ *The abandoned ruins of Garth Farm can be seen just beyond this impressive wall, built from locally quarried stone.*

THE CASTLE BY THE DUNES

14

A gentle walk across farmland to a ruined castle

The walk begins at the Church of St Teilo in the delightful village of Merthyr Mawr. This modest, mostly mid-19th-century building includes some older remains in its fabric. A sundial from 1720 graces the church wall, while the churchyard has a number of old tombs topped with recumbent figures, their hands clasped in prayer, that predate their surrounds.

The route leads through the village ❷, a scattering of houses spread out along the road. Many are thatched, some with wonderfully irregular roof lines and eyebrows of thatch above their upper windows.

▲ *The ruins of Candleston Castle stand in a woodland clearing by dunes where there were once extensive managed rabbit warrens. Pheasants (inset) are reared nearby and stalk the local fields.*

The old post office has a particularly interesting chimney, which appears halfway up the gable wall. It is worth exploring the village to admire its attractive houses, but the main walk turns off past the post office to follow the high wall surrounding the parkland of Merthyr-mawr House.

Along the way, the iron gateway to Home Farm looks exactly like those once used as tollgates on Welsh roads. Ornamental trees lean out over the park wall. From the rookeries here the air is filled with raucous cries, while pheasants inhabit the fields beside the road.

FIELDS AND WOODLAND

Having left Merthyr Mawr, you join a broad, rough track and there are views of the low hills to the north. Passing the whitewashed, slate-roofed Whitney Farm, the track gives way to a green lane, then bends round the edge of a patch of woodland and crosses fields by a series of stiles to the main road.

The busy A48 comes as a noisy, but very brief, intrusion, and almost immediately the route turns off over a stone stile through a hedge. This distinctive type of stile is very common in this part of the world. The route continues across grassy fields and through a small copse. Nearby is the site of an ancient enclosure and a long barrow. From this part of the walk there are good views back to Trelales (Laleston), with its prominent church tower, and to the hills beyond. Up ahead is the hamlet of Tythegston and the impressive buildings of Tythegston Court.

COUNTRY LANE

Tythegston's church, although usually locked, is reached by an attractive cobbled path. From the hamlet, the route follows a narrow country lane, bordered by hedgerows and trees, as it winds gently uphill.

Eventually this gives way to a rough farm track, leading to some sand dunes ❸. This attractive area has pine trees growing in the sandy soil. The dainty, pink-tinged sea bindweed and viper's bugloss, a lovely deep purple colour, can be found here. Just short of Candleston Farm, the route leaves the track for a stony path that runs down through

THE WALK

MERTHYR MAWR – CANDLESTON CASTLE

The walk begins by the church in Merthyr Mawr **Ⓐ**.

1 With your back to the church, turn left up the road. Where the road divides beyond the post box and old post office opposite, turn left.

2 Where the road turns right at the top of the hill, leave it to go straight on along a broad track. Ignore a footpath off to the right marked with a yellow arrow and continue past Whitney Farm.

3 Bear right into a field then go through a gate on your left, aiming for the boundary wall of some woods. Follow the wall to reach a stile.

4 Cross the stile and turn right to follow a hedge, crossing the fields over a series of stiles. At the road (A48) turn left.

5 Where power lines cross the hedge, look for a stone stile on your left. Cross it and go straight across the field towards a dead tree. Cross another

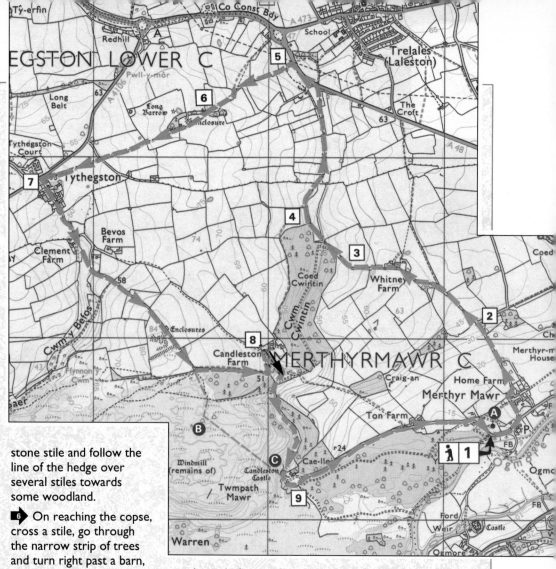

stone stile and follow the line of the hedge over several stiles towards some woodland.

6 On reaching the copse, cross a stile, go through the narrow strip of trees and turn right past a barn, following the path ahead across crop fields towards the buildings of Tythegston. At the last field before the hamlet, bear right to its corner to reach a road.

7 Turn left and follow the road, which becomes a

rough track, for nearly a mile (1.6km) to an area of dunes **Ⓑ**. Bear left with the track towards Candleston Farm. The track bends sharp left, then right as it approaches the farm.

8 At the right-hand bend

take a path to the right, going steeply downhill through some woodland. Continue for ½ mile (0.8km) to come to Candleston Castle **Ⓒ**.

9 Take the minor road to return to Merthyr Mawr.

woodland to an area of huge dunes.

The path ends at a car park beside Candleston Castle **Ⓒ**. The name is misleading as the 'castle' was actually a 14th-century fortified manor house, though today it stands in ruins. Some of the outer fortifications survive, but what remains of the house has a more domestic air. The dark basement area is crudely vaulted, but at first-floor level you can see the fireplace of the grand hall, with part of its intricately-carved stone surround. From here, the route follows a quiet country road back to Merthyr Mawr.

◀*Merthyr Mawr is a peaceful country village with quiet, stone-walled lanes and pleasant thatched cottages.*

A walk through hills and valleys in a post-industrial landscape

When the Countryside Act of 1968 gave money to local authorities to make country parks, efforts were made to return the Dare Valley, long disfigured by spoil heaps and rusting railway lines, to its original condition. The tips that overshadowed Cwmdare village were spread out over the valley floor, and the colliery machinery was dismantled and removed. Trees were planted and the River Dare, contained in a culvert, was brought back above ground to create lakes and waterfalls.

Dare Valley Country Park's visitor centre, where this walk begins, is built on the site of Powell's Pit. The stones for its walls and the cast-iron pillars inside were taken from redundant chapels in the area.

The route follows a tarmac road and turns off where a man-made waterfall cascades under a bridge into a pond. A sign indicates the route of the Coed Morgannwg Way, a long-distance footpath that starts

FACT FILE

- ✳ Cwmdare, 1 mile (1.6km) west of Aberdare
- 📇 Pathfinder 1108 (SN 80/90), grid reference SN 984026

  miles 0 1 2 3 4 5 6 7 8 9 10 miles
  kms 0 1 2 3 4 5 6 7 8 9 10 11 12 13 14 15 kms

- ◐ Allow 3½ hours
- ▬ Good walking on well defined paths, some of them muddy. Steady climbing for the first 2 miles (3.2km)
- P At the start
- 🍴 Café and toilets at the visitor centre
- I Dare Valley Country Park is open all year round. For times Tel. (01685) 883099

at Margam and continues for 36 miles (58km) to Gethin. Here there was once a hamlet, Pithead, that served the Merthyr Dare Colliery. Nothing remains of either site now, other than a few grass-covered spoil heaps up the hill on the left.

As you climb the slope into a

▲ *As the route climbs Craig Pen-rhiw-llêch, there is a good view over the reservoir to a terrace of cottages built for the workers of Bwllfa Colliery. The marsh thistle (inset) grows nearby.*

small wood, the route follows a sunken track **Ⓐ**. The stones underfoot and the drainage ditch to the side indicate that this is an example of a made-up parish road from before the coal mining era. This well preserved early route to Rhondda survived in its original state because other, more convenient roads were built, leaving this one to the walker.

EVOCATIVE RUINS

The ruined cottage **Ⓑ** on the left of the track at Pen-rhiw-llêch, abandoned in 1938, is a reminder of the system of farming whereby shepherds took their flocks to the high meadowland or 'hafod' in summer, and retreated to the shelter of the valleys in winter. There is additional evidence of this practice in a number of ruined dwellings on the surrounding hillsides.

There are woodpeckers in the scant woodland of birch, oak and elder; their holes can be seen in the tree trunks. On the steep slopes and

THE WALK

DARE VALLEY – TARREN Y BWLCH

The walk begins outside Dare Valley Country Park's visitor centre.

1 With the centre behind you, turn right along the road. Go through a metal gate and cross a stream by a bridge. Turn left before the bridge over the next stream, along a track marked 'Coed Morgannwg Way'. Swing left uphill, ignoring a right-hand path that follows the stream. The track becomes sunken **A** where it enters some trees, and follows the edge of the hill. Continue uphill, ignoring all turns to the left, past a ruined cottage **B**. Go over a stile to the top of Tarren y Bwllfa.

2 Follow the path to the right, along the rim of Tarren y Bwllfa, and cross a stream. Ignore the white-painted stones marking the point where the Coed Morgannwg Way turns left; continue for 100 yards (90m), then fork right along the edge of the cliff to Berw-ddu Waterfall **C**. Return to the fork and turn right along the track to the line of pylons. Turn right, following the yellow waymarkers along the line of the pylons to a wire fence. Go through a metal gate and continue along the track to the viewpoint **D**, which is almost at the edge of Tarren y Bwlch.

3 Retrace your steps for 50 yards (45m) to where a waymarker points you left, downhill. Follow a broad track past piles of stones **E** and, eventually, over a stile right of a metal gate.

4 Climb another stile and turn right, downhill, keeping the wall on your right. After 200 yards, where the wall ends, follow the path as it turns sharp left, downhill. About 50 yards (45m) before a pylon, turn sharp right. Continue downhill, passing a corrugated-iron pen on your right and a disused air shaft **F** on your left. Cross a stile onto the road.

5 Cross, and enter the Dare Valley Country Park by another stile. There are

◄Near the start of the walk, the water by the path crashes over man-made cascades that channel it into a pond.

open moorland, the mewing of the buzzard is a common sound, and ravens live here too. Peregrine falcons regularly hunt over the area.

As you climb higher, you can see rowan trees clinging precariously to gullies, a blaze of red berries in autumn. On the ground, nibbled by sheep, are bilberry plants. Two lakes are visible in the valley below; one is a reservoir, the other is part of the park's leisure facilities. They mark the site of Bwllfa Colliery, one of the largest in the area; nothing remains now except a row of cottages. To the left of Bwllfa Dare Terrace is Bwllfa House, which was originally a farm. When mining began, it became the property of the colliery manager, and, in due course, it was enlarged.

Ahead loom the steep cliffs of Tarren y Bwllfa. The hollowed-out shape was created by a glacier which formed on the north-facing slope. Bwllfa is one of the oldest place names in the district, and means 'basin' or 'site of a pool', suggesting that there may have been a glacial lake at the foot of the cliff.

The path emerges onto the flat land behind Tarren y Bwllfa and follows a narrow ridge of higher ground studded with granite outcrops. Beyond it, the land is boggy, and drains not into the Dare, as you would expect, but into the Rhondda Fach Valley to the south-west. On the left, in the distance, is the grass-covered dam of Lluest-wen Reservoir, with the darker green of conifer plantations beyond.

FOAMING FALLS

A quick detour takes you to the Berw-ddu Waterfall **C**, where the Dare drops over Tarren y Bwllfa. Berw-ddu means dark foaming' but it is only spectacular in very wet weather; normally, the moss absorbs the small amount of water.

The wet peaty soil supports marsh thistle, star sedge and creeping buttercup, while grasshoppers

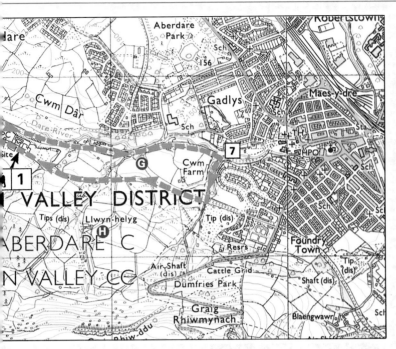

no paths here; walk to the lake straight ahead. Turn left at the picnic tables and walk between birch trees. A clear track emerges here. Follow it to the road.

6 Turn left and follow the road downhill for 50 yards (45m). Turn right at a boulder and take a tarmac path, which crosses a wooden bridge over waterfalls, with a lake on your left. After ½ mile (800m), the remains of Brunel's wooden viaduct **G** are visible where a gate on the left leads to a road down to the river. Continue along the path, through a wicket gate, for another ¼ mile (400m), to a grassy clearing beside the river, with picnic tables.

7 Before a bridge crosses a stream, turn right up a muddy path, which goes over one stream and keeps another on its left as it climbs uphill through woods. Pass under a bridge and a pipe, then turn right immediately, out of the cutting. Turn right again, over a stile onto a road. Turn left and follow the road back to the visitor centre, passing Llwyn-helyg farm **H** away to your left.

▲ *The view north from Tarren y Bwlch stretches over Tower Colliery to the Brecon Beacons, 12 miles (19km) away.*

▼ *From near the visitor centre, there is a tempting prospect of what the walk has in store. The top of Tarren y Bwllfa gives a fine view (above) of the Dare Valley.*

and frogs are found among the clumps of purple moor-grass.

The route heads north and passes a trig point marking the summit of these hills, at 1,672 feet (510m). At the clifftop of Tarren y Bwlch, the view **D** is superb. On a clear day, the distinctive outline of the Brecon Beacons can be seen on the horizon. In the foreground is the town of Hirwaun, and immediately below is Tower Colliery, the last operative mine in the South Wales coalfield.

Just beneath the cliffs is evidence of a prehistoric settlement. As you go downhill on a broad track, you pass pre-Roman rock cairns **E**. The sheep pen in the middle of these is 18th-century in origin, but archaeologists have identified a prehistoric settlement nearby, of 17 round huts and enclosures.

A winding path takes you to the edge of Cwmdare village. It passes to the right of a mound of grass-covered stones with a concrete plug at their centre. This is a disused air shaft **F**, one of many that served the underground tunnels in the area.

ALONG THE DARE

The route crosses the country park almost to the start of the walk, but turns left to join a tarmac path, lined with oak, elder and birch trees, that heads along the river towards Aberdare. The Dare was once a source of fascination to local people; at one spot, flammable gas seeped up through the water, making it

Mining in Cwmdare

The coal seams of the Welsh valleys were formed when layers of rotting vegetation from vast forests were covered by sediment from the invading sea in a cycle that repeated itself many times. Eventually, the weight of the subsequent layers changed the peat into coal and the sediment into shale and sandstone.

One of the first mines in this area was worked by a farmer at Pen-rhiw-llêch, in the 1750s. He employed one or two men, and the coal was largely for his own use. In the latter half of the 18th century, Lord Mountstuart, later the Marquis of Bute, who owned land to the north of Cwmdare, granted leases to anyone wanting to mine coal or iron. Many worked primitive, open-cast mines known as 'patches'. Some of these were still in existence in the 1920s, when miners used them during strikes to dig coal for their families.

It was in the 1850s that coalmining began in earnest in the

This pithead winding gear is all that remains of Bwllfa Dare Colliery, which was cleared to make way for a country park.

Dare Valley. Between 1855 and 1864, four pits were opened — at Merthyr Dare, Bwllfa Dare, Cwmdare and Nantmelin. By 1900, these collieries were largely the property of the Llewellyn family. The Llewellyns lived locally, in Bwllfa House, and owned other independent collieries, such as Llwynhelyg and Windber. By the 1930s, they possessed most of the coal in the valley. In 1933, 3,000 men worked in the Cwmdare mines alone.

The economic depression before

World War II tooks its toll. Between 1935 and 1940, all but one of the collieries closed; the Nantmelin Pit was finally abandoned in 1947.

A bid to restore Bwllfa Dare Colliery was made in the 1950s, when it was linked up underground with the Maerdy Pit in Rhondda Fach, but it closed again in 1977, though the shaft was kept open until 1989.

In 1991, all the mine buildings were removed to make way for the Dare Valley Country Park. Today, a small section of pithead gear standing alone by the lake is all that remains of an industry that dominated the valley for nearly 100 years.

possible to 'set the river on fire'.

The walk follows the course of the old Taff Vale railway line, which opened in 1863, and took coal from the Bwllfa Colliery to Dare Valley Junction in Aberdare, where it joined the main line to Cardiff Docks. The line closed in 1959 and was made into a footpath.

BRUNEL'S VIADUCT

After ½ mile (800m), there are some brick pillars **G**, overgrown with ivy and ferns. These are all that remain of a wooden viaduct built by Isambard Kingdom Brunel to take another line across the river. It was 450 feet (137m) long and 70 feet (21m) high, and a scale model of it can be seen in the visitor centre. The

◄*The path follows the River Dare through some attractive woodland.*

viaduct was dismantled in 1947; only its supports were left standing.

Brunel was responsible for the Dare Aman railway, which you follow on the return route. The path passes under a bridge and a pipe, the remnants of Dare Junction station, which was situated here.

The line, of which the viaduct was a part, was in competition with the Taff Vale line, although there is evidence that it carried timber and supplies rather than coal. It was initially constructed in broad gauge so that it could link up with the South Wales Railway, but had to be

reduced to standard gauge when it became part of the Great Western Railway. Between 1906 and 1924, the Dare Aman line carried passengers; it was closed to all traffic in 1939.

This return route passes a sign to Llwyn-helyg farm **H**. According to tradition, a plant grew in the fields here that made cattle vicious if they ate it. It must have had some effect on humans too, for in 1868 Thomas Morris from Aberaman stole some gunpowder from a local pit and attempted to blow up the farm. Although the house was damaged, no one was injured. Later, the land was mined, and the old spoil heaps of Llwyn-helyg Colliery can be seen beside the road.

▶*These brick supports, covered with ferns and ivy, are all that remain of a soaring wooden railway viaduct that was built over the River Dare by the engineer Isambard Kingdom Brunel.*

PRINCE SILIAN'S CAVE

16

Bristol Channel. He established the first Christian university in Britain and it became famous throughout North Europe. Some of his more famous students included Taliesin, the Welsh bard; St Samson, the Archbishop of Dol; St Gildas, the historian; and St David, patron saint of Wales. The monastery flourished until the Romans arrived, when it became a cell of Tewkesbury Abbey.

The present church of St Illtud **B** dates back to the 13th century and it contains some interesting inscribed stones and Celtic crosses. One of the many interesting memorials is a stone recording the death of

◀ *A romantic setting for a wedding: Tresilian Cave was used for marriages until an Act of Parliament was passed in the mid-18th century forbidding this. The stone arch (below) inside the Cave.*

A bracing coastal walk to visit a romantic cave

Starting from an historic settlement, which at one time was famous as a monastic seat of learning, this short, easy walk follows lanes and tracks through farmland. It then leads to the Glamorgan Heritage Coast to enjoy the bracing air and the smell of the sea.

The history of Llantwit Major **A** goes back to Roman times. The old Welsh name for the place is Llanilltud Fawr, which was gradually corrupted over the passing years to Llantwit Major.

HISTORIC BUILDINGS

Narrow streets twist and turn in all directions and there are many interesting buildings. Two examples are the two-storey, medieval Town Hall, whose foundations date back to the 13th century, and the Old Swan Inn, which was where the judges (who held courts in the Town Hall) used to stay.

According to legend, the first church here was founded by Eurgain, a daughter of the Celtic chieftain, Caractacus, but it was

FACT FILE

✴ Llantwit Major, on the junction of the B4265 and the B4270, 15 miles (24 km) south-west of Cardiff, South Glamorgan

▭ Pathfinder 1163 (SS 87/96/97), grid reference SS 966687

miles 0 1 2 3 4 5 6 7 8 9 10 miles
kms 0 1 2 3 4 5 6 7 8 9 10 11 12 13 14 15 kms

◔ Allow 3 hours

▭ An easy walk involving very little ascent. Children should not walk too close to the cliff top on the section of Heritage Coast Walk

P In the centre of Llantwit Major at a car park near the old Town Hall, which overlooks the church

WC In Llantwit Major

🍴 Pubs, cafés, pubs, restaurants and shops in Llantwit Major

destroyed by Irish pirates. In the 6th century, the Breton St Illtud settled here and established his mud-and-wattle church in a hollow, hoping that it would not be seen by the pirates who sailed up and down the

Matthew Voss, at the great age of 129 years in 1534.

The bay and the cave of Tresilian **C** are named after Prince Silian, who was said to be one of the earliest converts to Christianity and later became known as St Silian. A large house on the edge of the bay is reputed to stand on the site of his

THE WALK

LLANTWIT MAJOR –TRESILIAN CAVE

The walk starts from a car park in the centre of Llantwit Major ⒶⒶ near the Town Hall.

1 From near the entrance to the car park, go down the lane behind the Job Centre. On reaching a junction, bear right and shortly you will reach St Illtud's Church Ⓑ.

2 After visiting the ancient church, continue along the lane and shortly ascend some steps on the left. Then turn left to go past a terrace of cottages. Ignore the steps on the left about half-way down the lane. Soon the lane narrows to a path. At a corner, go right over a stone stile and continue through the next field to reach another stile in the corner by the field.

3 Continue along Church Lane, which is flanked by high hedges. It ends at a stone stile. Beyond this, continue through three fields, keeping the hedge on your left, and cross another stile.

4 At the end of the last field, go over a stile and then immediately left over a stone/metal stile. Follow a path that leads down towards the sea through a shallow valley.

5 On reaching the coastal path turn right and follow it along the clifftop keeping well back from the edge. Shortly, on the right, you will pass a war-time gun emplacement post that has been preserved as a relic of those times. It is unusual, being constructed in stone. Around the next corner you will see the large entrance to Tresilian Cave Ⓒ in the cliff opposite, facing the sea.

6 Descend some steps and walk across the pebbles and rocks of Tresilian Bay (depending on the tidal conditions) to reach the cave entrance. After visiting the cave, retrace your steps along the coastal path to go past the shallow valley (mentioned in Stage 4) and continue along the coastal path, crossing a stone stile on the way.

7 On reaching the top of some steps, go left and follow a path heading inland, overlooking Cwm Col-huw Ⓓ. On the headland opposite is the site of a promontory fort Ⓔ. Go over a stone stile and up some steps to join a broader track. Soon you will see Llantwit Major in the distance at the head of the valley. Carry on past farm buildings and follow track and road.

8 At the end of Flanders Road, turn left at a T-junction. Then follow the lane between stone walls and turn right to arrive back at the starting point.

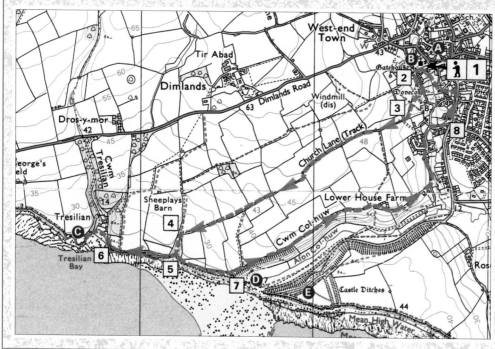

4th-century court. Another building that used to stand on this spot was a farmhouse, which also served as an inn frequented by smugglers and wreckers.

BOW OF DESTINY

Tresilian cave has romantic associations. Inside the cave is a natural arch, which stretches across the cavern about 4 feet (1.2 metres) below its roof. It is known as the 'bow of destiny'. Lovers who wished to find out how long it would be before they married used to come here. The man would try to throw a round pebble over the arch so that it fell to the other side without touching the rock arch or the roof of the cave. The number of tries he made before succeeding indicated the number of years the couple would have to wait before they married. Runaway marriages used to take place in the cave and at one time it became known as St Silian's, as if it were a church.

On Col-huw Point, overlooking the old harbour, are the remains of a promontory fort Ⓔ, established with triple earthworks to defend the coast from invasion and St Illtud may well have landed in the tiny creek of Cwm Col-huw Ⓓ, disembarking on a jetty built by Roman masons.

▼*St Illtud's church houses several interesting memorial stones and has a big collection of carved Celtic crosses.*

THE FAIRY-TALE CASTLE

17

▲ *From its romantic setting on a hillside above the Taff valley, Castell Coch offers a magnificent view to any passer-by. The surrounding woods are the habitat of the woodmouse (inset).*

A hilltop walk taking in the woods surrounding Castell Coch

The walk begins at the magnificent mock medieval castle of Castell Coch, the 'Red Castle', and most of the route leads through attractive, broad-leaved woodland.

Castell Coch **A** is one of the most extraordinary buildings in Britain. There was a castle on the site, but when the third Marquess of Bute decided on its 'restoration' in the late 19th century it was a complete ruin. He turned to the American architect William Burges, with whom he had already worked on the rebuilding of Cardiff Castle. An enthusiastic medievalist, Burges set about building this magnificent edifice, though its array of round turrets might look more at home overlooking the Rhine rather than the River Taff. It is well worth spending time here, for the interior is, if anything, even more sumptuous than the exterior.

TRACES OF THE PAST

The first part of the walk passes through the forest, still dominated by broad-leaved trees, particularly beech and birch, instead of the popular conifers. On either side of the track you can see curious humps and hollows, suggesting that at some time in the past there must have been mining or quarrying in this area.

The woodland path ends, but the walk remains very much in a woodland setting. For a short way, it follows a quiet country road, where it is accompanied by a noisily splashing stream, then the route turns back to footpaths and bridleways. There is a brief walk along the pavement to the attractive Travellers Rest pub of pinkwashed stone and thatch, before you turn back on to a minor road, and then head off again for a footpath across the fields. Here

▼ *The banqueting hall's special attractions are its solid stone chimney-piece and murals on the end walls.*

FACT FILE

✳ Castell Coch, just north-west of Tongwynlais, South Glamorgan

🗺 Pathfinder 1148 (ST 08/18), grid reference ST 131826

miles 0 · 1 · 2 · 3 · 4 · 5 · 6 · 7 · 8 · 9 · 10 miles
kms 0 · 1 · 2 · 3 · 4 · 5 · 6 · 7 · 8 · 9 · 10 · 11 · 12 · 13 · 14 · 15 kms

◔ Allow 3 hours

▭ Fairly easy on good, clear paths, but can be muddy in places

P Castell Coch, signposted from A470

T Cardiff to Tongwynlais by bus

🍺 Public house on A469 (stage 8 on map)

THE WALK

CASTELL COCH

The walk starts at the car park at Castell Coch ⓐ.

▶**1** With your back to the castle you will see two paths through the woods. Take the path that curves

steeply uphill, waymarked by a sign with three red castles.

▶**2** At the top of the hill, turn right on to the broad track, as indicated by the white arrow opposite. This brings you out on to a wide

forest track. It passes the disused pit ⓑ and a golf course.

▶**3** At the road turn right.

▶**4** Just beyond the point where the road crosses the stream, turn left to cross

the stream at the footbridge, and cross the stile on the left to take the path going steeply uphill.

▶**5** At the broad track turn left and where the path divides to create steps made out of widely spaced, wooden slats take the right-hand fork.

▶**6** At the road turn right, then immediately left by public footpath sign and keep to the broad track to the left past the houses.

▶**7** At the road turn right, slightly uphill.

▶**8** Turn right on to the minor road opposite the

Travellers Rest pub.

▶**9** At the gateway to Wenallt Farm, cross the stile on the left and follow the arrows across the fields to the woodland, as indicated by the arrows with views across the valley ⓒ. The path continues into the woodland.

▶**10** Where the path divides take the fork beside the wire fence.

▶**11** At the wooden section of fence you can look across to the stream on your right. Cross the fence and the stream by the stepping stones and continue up to the left.

▶**12** At the road turn right.

▶**13** At the top of the hill ignore the first large public footpath sign. Look for small, yellow-arrowed footpath sign and turn left. Follow the footpath — not the bridleway — round the edge of the woodland.

▶**14** Cross the footbridge and carry straight on across the road on the footpath opposite. Continue to follow the well-defined path with wooden borders which comes out at the driveway immediately below the car park at Castell Coch.

ⓒ are some of the best views of the walk, looking out across the deep, wooded valley.

The route back to the start is barred by the little river at the bottom of the valley, but this is easily crossed at the small ford via conveniently placed stones. From here the path runs up past the side of a small reservoir to join the last short road section of the walk. Turning off the

road, back on to the footpath, brings you once again into the woods and you emerge at the end of the walk at the driveway of Castell Coch, looking up at the tall round towers.

◀*Lush greenery and wildflowers line the little river that must be crossed during the walk. Inside the castle, the drawing room boasts a splendid, high-domed ceiling (right).*

A CASTLE AND CLIFFS

18

▲*The coastal path runs along cliffs that are divided into many strata. The adder (inset) may be seen around here but, though a poisonous snake, it will only bite when it is cornered.*

FACT FILE

- ✳ Nash Point on the Glamorgan Heritage Coastal Path, 4 miles (6.4km) west of Llantwit Major

- ▦ Pathfinder 1163 (SS 87/96/97), grid reference SS 916684

  miles 0 1 2 3 4 5 6 7 8 9 10 miles
  kms 0 1 2 3 4 5 6 7 8 9 10 11 12 13 14 15 kms

- ◔ Allow 3 hours

- ▭ Two wooded valleys, roads, tracks and a clifftop path. Parts can be very muddy after rain

- Ⓟ Nash Point car park

- ⑪ Cabin selling soft drinks and ice cream at car park (closed in winter). Pub at Marcross, 1 mile (1.6km) to north-east

Through a valley to two churches and a castle, returning along cliffs

This varied walk takes in a section of the Glamorgan Heritage Coastal Path and provides an opportunity to see Atlantic College, housed in an impressive castle, and two interesting churches.

It begins with a walk up a wooded valley to Marcross, whose church Ⓐ was constructed in the 12th century. It was extended in the 14th century, with the addition of a chancel and a tower with a 'saddle back' roof. The Norman font in the nave is decorated with cable moulding.

▼*St Donat's Castle is usually open on Sundays. The film* Citizen Kane *was based on Hearst, who owned the castle.*

THE WALK

NASH POINT – ST DONAT'S

The walk starts from the car park at Nash Point, reached by a lane from Marcross.

1 From the car park, follow a stony track into the valley and up through it, bearing left at a junction and crossing several small streams on stepping stones. (After heavy rain it is best to follow the road.)

2 Cross a small footbridge, then turn left up some steps. Go over a stile and continue through the field. Just before a house, go right through a gate and left up the road. Marcross Church **A** is on your left. Turn right at the T-junction by the Horseshoe Inn.

3 Keep right at the next junction, walking uphill, and take the second farm track on the right.

4 Follow the lane to Parc Farm. On reaching a junction, turn right and go through a wooden pedestrian gate.

5 Follow a grass track (it can be muddy) through the trees, passing through a wire gate and keeping left at a junction. The path leads through a secluded valley to a clearing and a ruined cottage. Turn right at the lane ahead to visit St Donat's Church **B**.

6 Return up the lane, with the boundary wall of St Donat's Castle **C** on your right. Further on you join the castle driveway.

7 Turn right at the road and follow it for about 600 yards (550m).

8 Turn off right through a metal kissing gate with crests at either side, and follow a path down the side of King George's Field, with woodland on your right, to a gate.

9 Turn right through the gate along the coastal path, passing along the southernmost boundary of Atlantic College and over an RNLI slipway.

10 Go up the steps to the right and through the trees. Bear left at the top, down five wooden steps and over a stone stile to rejoin the clifftop path, passing Nash Point lighthouse on your way back to the car park.

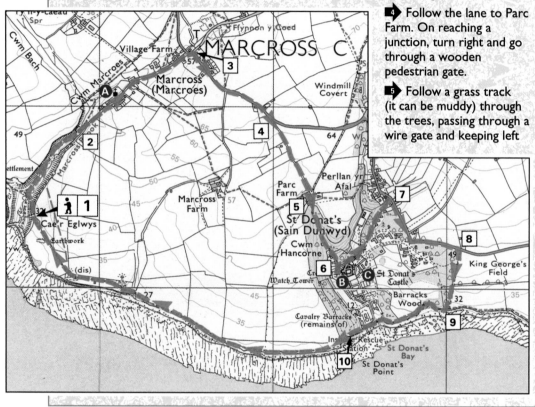

From Marcross, the route follows a road and a farm track to a wooded valley below St Donat's Castle. Past a clearing with a ruined cottage is St Donat's Church **B**, an ancient but modest building which has benefited from the patronage of the Stradling family, whose chapel contains many fine tombs. On the south side of the churchyard there is a late 15th-century cross, carved with an image of the crucifixion.

MILLIONAIRE'S CASTLE

The walk then skirts the grounds of St Donat's Castle **C**, for 500 years the seat of the Stradling family. In 1925 it was acquired by the American newspaper millionaire, William Randolph Hearst, who spent a fortune on restoring it but in the following years spent only one month there. Since 1962 the castle has been known as Atlantic College, and accommodates 300 young men and women of sixth-form age from all over the world.

The final part of the walk follows the clifftop, with good views up and down the coast and across the Bristol Channel towards Exmoor. The path dips down at St Donat's Bay, where there is a lifeboat station, and later passes two lighthouses, the second of them disused.

▶ *The view east along the Glamorgan Heritage Coastal Path from near Barracks Wood. Views in all directions are spectacular, but keep children or dogs away from the edge, as it is liable to crumble.*

WAVES ACROSS THE WAVES

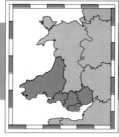

A Victorian resort, and a country park with an unexpected attraction

Penarth grew up around a tiny church on a headland overlooking Cardiff Bay. In the 19th century, the medieval St Augustine's was replaced by a much grander church, designed by William Butterfield. A fashionable town, home to several ship- and mineowners, developed on the headland, while a genteel seaside resort grew up southwards along the coast.

A pier ❹ was built there in 1894, and a regular steamship service was established between Clevedon, in Somerset, and Penarth. The pier is still used for steamship sailings today, including the *Waverley*, the last sea-going paddle steamer in the world. It also provides the starting

▲The coast path provides sweeping views back to Penarth, dominated by the parish church on Penarth Head. The reed warbler (inset) can be heard in the reed beds at Cosmeston Lakes.

point for the walk, which soon climbs the hill behind the esplanade, into Windsor Gardens. This strip of lawns and shrubbery, complete with bandstand, was laid out in 1884, and retains an air of quiet gentility.

VIEWS OF SOMERSET

A clifftop path, running first through wide lawns, and then along a gravel track between hedges and fields, gives fine views across the Severn Estuary; beyond the islands of Flat Holm and Steep Holme are Clevedon, Sand Bay and Brean Down, with the Mendips rising

▼Near Lavernock, the distinct strata of the cliffs reveal the area's geology.

behind. Further south are Brent Knoll and the Quantocks.

The coastal path ends, somewhat abruptly, at Lavernock ❺. If the tide allows, you may like to go down to the beach and scramble across the stones to Lavernock Point. From the pavement of limestone beneath the cliffs there are splendid views across the Bristol Channel to Exmoor.

Lavernock today consists of a few

FACT FILE

- Penarth, 3 miles (4.8km) south of Cardiff, on the A4160

- Pathfinder 1180 (ST 06/16), grid reference ST 189713

miles 0	1	2	3	4	5	6	7	8	9	10 miles
kms 0	1 2 3 4 5 6 7 8	9 10 11 12 13 14 15 kms								

- Allow 2½ hours

- Level walking on good paths and tracks

- **P** Several car parks in Penarth, including a free long-stay car park at the end of Cliff Parade

- Full range of facilities in Penarth. Cafeteria at Cosmeston Lakes Country Park Visitor Centre

- **I** Penarth Tourist Information Centre by the pier has details of the country park's opening times, and of the tours to the medieval village, Tel. (01222) 708849

THE WALK

PENARTH – LAVERNOCK

The walk begins by the pier ⓐ in Penarth.

1 Walk along the front, the sea on your left, to the lifeboat station, about 100 yards (90m) along on your right. Go through the gate and bear left. Climb the iron steps on your right to the roof. Turn left up the concrete steps to Windsor Gardens. Turn left. Continue through the gates and over a crossing path that leads down to the front. At the end of the gardens, bear left around the brick lodge to a road.

2 Cross and turn right to pick up the path running to the left of the shelter. Continue along the clifftop for just over 1½ miles (2.4km), to Lavernock ⓑ.

3 Turn right past an abandoned farm house and chapel, along a narrow winding road. At a T-junction, cross the busy road with care and climb a gate opposite. Go ahead to the stile opposite. Cosmeston medieval village ⓒ is on your right.

4 Climb the stile and turn right. The track soon leads between two old quarry pits that are now lakes ⓓ. Cross a bridge. After 50 paces, turn right and follow the path around the lake to your right. Cosmeston Lakes Country Park Visitor Centre ⓔ is off to the right. Continue to the main gate.

5 Cross the road and turn left. Take the first right, Cosmeston Drive, and follow it for nearly ¼ mile (400m). About 20 paces beyond Althorp Drive, near the top of a rise, turn left down a gravel track. Continue as this becomes a road. Turn left by the chestnut trees and continue ahead, under the bridge, on the railway path.

6 Where the path opens out into a verge by a road, turn right down Alberta Place. Continue ahead down Alberta Road to a five-way junction. Take the second left, and follow it as it bears left down the seafront to the start.

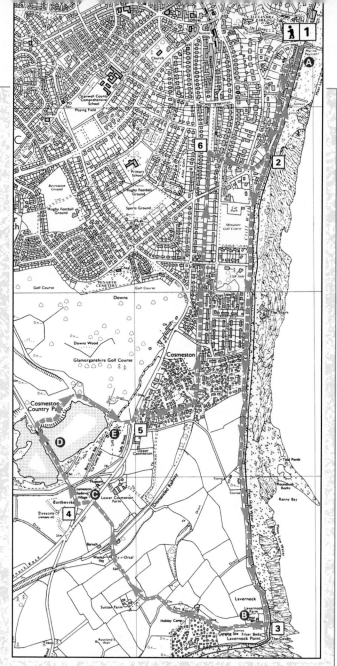

◄ *At Cosmeston, a medieval village is being reconstructed, down to details such as this ancient breed of goat.*

ruined farm buildings and a small church. In the farm, on 11 May 1897, Marconi received the first radio message ever transmitted across water, when his colleague on Flat Holm prosaically asked 'Are you ready?'. A plaque on the churchyard wall commemorates this event.

A lane leads past the chalets of the Marconi Country Club to Cosmeston ⓒ. This is the site of a village deserted in the 14th century and rediscovered only in 1982. Excavations continue, and the village is slowly being reconstructed on the original foundations using medieval tools, methods and materials.

LAKELAND PARK

The village is within the boundaries of Cosmeston Lakes Country Park, created on the site of some limestone quarries. The route leads along an old lane between the lakes ⓓ. The one on the right is used for windsurfing and sailing, while that on the left is a conservation area; its islands of reeds and sedges provide nesting places for waterbirds.

The route goes around the pleasure lake and past the visitor centre ⓔ, which has displays on the park's wildlife, and provides guided tours of the medieval village.

At the main entrance, you cross the main Penarth to Sully road into a modern housing estate built on the site of an old limeworks. A road leads gently uphill to what was once a railway branch line, and is now a footpath leading back into Penarth through the extensive modern development south of the town.

The walk ends with a stroll along the seafront back to the pier. On the way, you pass the ornate Victorian iron verandahs of the Yacht Club and the formal Italian Gardens, which were laid out in 1926.

RHOSSILI BAY

FACT FILE

- ✳ Rhossili, Gower peninsula, about 15 miles (24 km) west of Swansea off A4118

- 🗺 Pathfinders 1145 (SS 48/58/68), and 1126 (SS 49/59), grid reference SS 414881

  miles 0 1 2 3 4 5 6 7 8 9 10 miles
  kms 0 1 2 3 4 5 6 7 8 9 10 11 12 13 14 15 kms

- ◔ Allow 2 hours

- ▭ Easy, apart from a sharp ascent from the bay to the down

- P Rhossili car park

- 🍴 Refreshments at Rhossili and shop at caravan site (open Easter to end October)

- WC Toilets at Rhossili and caravan site

A seaside walk around a beautiful bay on the Gower peninsula

The great sweep of Rhossili Bay — 3 miles (4.8 km) of firm, golden sand scoured by Atlantic rollers — is a breathtaking sight for those who venture to the most westerly point of the Gower peninsula. This is one of the finest stretches of unspoiled beach in Britain, and it is now under the protection of the National Trust, which has a visitor centre ⓐ near the car park at the start of this walk.

The centre contains much information about Gower past and present, and also displays the times of the tides. It is essential to check these times before setting off on a walk as both beach and shingle can be covered at high water. Care must also be taken when walking over the rocks as they can be very slippery and dangerous.

THE NORMAN INFLUENCE

The peninsula offers walkers peace and quiet, and an abundance of natural beauty. Warlike Norman

▲ *The spectacular bay of Rhossili stretches 3 miles (4.8 km) from Worms Head. (inset) Guillemots nest in colonies on cliff edges near their marine food supply. A pair will lay only one egg.*

invaders exercised the strongest historical influence on Gower. Their triumph over Welsh resurgence, including that of Owain Glyndwr's revolt between 1400 and 1413, is characterised by the castles they built, which can still be seen today. At Rhossili there are also notable examples of the ancient open field system of cultivation, practised extensively in the peninsula after being introduced by West Country settlers. This system is known locally as the *viel* (pronounced 'vile').

A SERPENT OF LAND

The walk continues along the bay and offers fine views back towards Worms Head ⓑ, a serpent-like promontory, which is Gower's most westerly point and now a bird sanctuary — a haven for guillemot, razorbill and kittiwake, as well as occasional migrants such as whimbrel, ring ouzel, grey wagtail and wryneck. Worms Head can be reached on foot at low tide (see

coastguard notice for times) and makes an interesting excursion for another day.

Although Gower's climate is mild, powerful westerly gales have wrecked ships here in the past. The skeleton of the *Helvetia* ⓒ, driven ashore in 1887, still shows above the sand. The most famous wreck was that of the South American 'Dollar Ship'. In 1807, and again in 1833, quantities of Peruvian dollars, dating from the reign of Philip IV, were

*The stark skeleton of the wreck **Helvetia**, buried in the sand.*

THE WALK

RHOSSILI — HILLEND — RHOSSILI DOWN

The walk begins from the car park at the end of the main road into Rhossili.

1 From the National Trust visitor centre **A**, follow the signposted path opposite the car park entrance, past the Worms Head Hotel down to the beach. With Worms Head promontory **B** behind you, walk northwards along the sandy bay, keeping Rhossili Down above on the right and passing the wreck of the *Helvetia* **C** on the left. Continue along the beach for about 2 miles (3.2 km).

2 Turn right on to a fenced path through the dunes. Turn right and head for a road leading through a caravan site.

3 On reaching a small shop, go through a gate on the right past a National Trust sign. Take the path to the top of the hill, then follow it down past Sweyne's Houses **D** to the triangulation pillar on Rhossili Hill Beacon **E**.

4 Walk down the hill to Rhossili, going through a gate at the bottom which leads to a road. Turn right and return to car park.

This 4000-year-old burial mound on Rhossili Down is thought to belong to a Scandinavian sealord.

uncovered by the tide. These were thought to be part of the dowry of a Portuguese princess. It is believed that some of the treasure is still buried in the sands of Rhossili.

A CHANGE OF SCENE

Turning inland at the dunes, the character of the walk changes completely. Sandy hummocks give way to open, grassy downland and larks rather than gulls wheel through the sky overhead.

On reaching the high ground of Rhossili Down, look out for two megalithic burial chambers **D** known as Sweyne's Houses. Legend has it that this is the burial place of Sweyne, a Scandinavian sealord who may have given his name to Swansea around 4000 BC.

Further on, Rhossili Hill Beacon **E**, at 632 feet (190 metres) the highest point in Gower, offers views to Lundy Island and the Devon coastline on a clear day.

ABERDULAIS FALLS

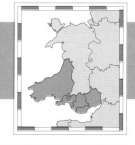

Spectacular waterfalls, a site of historic interest, woodland and hills

At first sight this is a typical South Wales valley, with its terraced houses and no fewer than three chapels huddled together looking, somewhat disapprovingly it seems, at the pub across the road. Crowded into the narrow valley floor are the main road, the railway and the Neath and Tenant Canal. Yet just across the road you step straight into as romantic and wild a scene as you could wish to find. From the road bridge you can see the solitary remaining arch of an older bridge across the River Dulais.

RENOVATION SCHEME

Aberdulais Falls **Ⓐ** and their surroundings are now in the care of the National Trust and a major renovation scheme was completed in 1991. Walkways provide splendid views of the falls and of the complex remains of the iron and tin plate works of the last century, while

FACT FILE

✳ Aberdulais, West Glamorgan, off the A365

▣ Pathfinders 1107 (SN 60/70) and 1127 (SS 69/79), grid reference SS 771993

miles 0 1 2 3 4 5 6 7 8 9 10 miles
kms 0 1 2 3 4 5 6 7 8 9 10 11 12 13 14 15 kms

◔ Allow 3 hours

▭ Moderately easy going on good paths

🅿 Aberdulais Falls Car Park

🆃 Bus from Swansea to Aberdulais, alight at Tonna, ½ mile (800 metres) from the start of the walk

🍴 Full range of facilities, including food, drink and public toilets, at Aberdulais

▲ *Aberdulais Falls crash down through the rugged gorge in a torrent of foam. Intertwining, writhing masses of brook lampreys (right) seen at spawning time.*

explanatory boards help the visitor to make sense of the site. There is something here for everyone: historical remains in a beautiful setting. The Information Centre has details of the industrial site on the ground

footpath with wooden steps.

5 At the top of the steps, turn right to follow the path by the wooden railings, waymarked by white dots on trees.

6 Where the path divides near houses, turn left to follow the zig-zag path up the hillside. At the broad track turn right, and continue on this path until you arrive at the edge of the woodland.

7 At the edge of the wood, cross the stile by the yellow arrow. At the field continue uphill as indicated by the arrow. You eventually reach a broad green track going uphill. The path continues to be waymarked. Across the valley is the old mine chimney **D**. Near the brow of the hill approaching the farm look out for a stone wall pierced by an arch **E**.

8 When you reach the white farm gate, turn right onto the broad farm track, past the farm buildings of

Gelli-march Farm.

9 At the roadway turn left. Where the road swings to the left, continue on the roadway leading down to the woodland; do not take the broad track that goes straight on.

10 At the point just past the entrance to the golf club and after the old limekiln **F**, where the stream goes under the road, turn left to go over the stile by the footpath sign. Inside the woodland, where the path divides by a stile, take the right-hand path leading past the wooden bench.

11 At the broad track turn left. By two posts, one marked in red, the other green, turn right to follow the narrow path, which turns right again to go steeply downhill. At the foot of the steps turn left onto the broad path and follow this to the main track at Stage 5, and retrace your steps to the start of the walk.

ABERDULAIS FALLS

The walk starts at the Aberdulais Falls car park on the A465 opposite the Dulais Rock Inn.

1 Cross the main road at the pedestrian crossing and turn right for the Falls **A**. After visiting the Falls, return to the main road.

2 Turn right to take the footpath up the steps,

almost opposite the Post Office, signposted to the Wild Life Park.

3 At the roadway turn right, passing the entrance to the Penscynor Wild Life Park **B**.

4 Turn left by the sign 'Welcome to the Vale of Neath Country Park: Craig Gwladys Woodlands'. At the woodland **C** continue straight on along the

floor and reproductions of some of the works of artists who came here, including J. M. W. Turner.

After leaving the falls, the walk climbs steeply up the hillside, arriving almost immediately at a country lane. Bordered by a hedge on one side and a stone wall on the other, the path leads past a farmyard,

◄ *From the road bridge you can see the solitary remaining arch of an older bridge across the River Dulais. The path leads through the varied trees of Craig Gwadys Woodlands (below).*

crosses the railway and arrives at the main road and the entrance to the Penscynor Wild Life Park **B**. The cries of exotic birds ring out over the valley and through the wire fence you can see some of the inhabitants ranging from deer to tropical birds. Beyond the park, you can see woodland **C** stretching round the hillside with a craggy crest rising above it. The path now leads up into this woodland, which is laced with a network of waymarked footpaths.

VARIED WOODLAND

Although at first the woodland is dominated by conifers there is none of the dense uniformity associated with so many modern forestry plantations. The tree cover is broken up by streams rushing down the hillside and rocks burst through the undergrowth so that the scenery is constantly changing. The walks have been skillfully devised to fit in with their surroundings, with log steps held in place by wooden pegs, simple, rustic railings, and seats and shelters made out of split logs. The woodland itself is varied and there is an incursion of birch into the otherwise relentless pine.

VALE OF NEATH

As you climb higher up the hill, so the rocks become a more dominant feature. Along the way, there are glimpses of the scenery of the Vale of Neath and the hills beyond. Towards the end of the woodland section, a greater variety of trees appears,

▲ *This wooden bench beside the rushing water makes a pleasant, if probably damp, resting place for weary walkers.*

including beech and oak.

When the woods end, the walk brings you out to a hillside of rough grassland, bracken and gorse. There are reminders here of the industrial past of the region — the grassy mounds of spoil heaps can be seen and across the valley by the pylons is the chimney ❶ of an old mine. The overall effect, though, is of remote hill scenery.

RUGGED SCENERY

The further you climb, the rougher and more rugged the scenery becomes — trees are bent by the wind, boulders scatter the hillside and dry stone walls straggle away to the horizon, and the view steadily opens out over rolling countryside. An unusual feature can be seen near the brow of the hill at Gelli-march

▲ *From the vantage point of a stile along the way, the view through the trees steadily opens out onto rolling countryside — a patchwork of fields divided by stone walls.*

▶ *Look out for the interesting details on this walk. Just before the route reaches Gelli-march Farm, there is a stone wall with a small arch in it to allow livestock through.*

Farm, where a dry stone wall has been pierced by an arch ❸ to allow the livestock through.

The return to Aberdulais begins on a country lane, that runs between dry stone walls, which are themselves interesting — the walls are topped by large, overhanging, flat slabs, kept in place by a haphazard jumble of heavy stones. This seems to be a very remote area, where the grassland is broken up only by areas of reedy marsh.

Over to the right, you can see a very simple, four-square, stone farmhouse in a shelter of trees and stone walls. There is such a strong sense of remoteness that it comes as something of a shock to find the road running round the boundary of Neath Golf Course. Yet the well-tended course has little impact — the scenery is still dominated by grasses, gorse and straggles of pine.

WOODLAND WATERFALLS

The road crosses a busy hill stream and runs down through attractive woodland. The water rushes on down the steep slope through a succession of gurgling falls, while the trees that crowd in are very different from those of the Craig Gwladys woods, for among the conifers are large, mature oak and beech. Here, too, there are spoil heaps from old mine workings.

On the left-hand side of the road, just by the entrance to the golf club, is an old limekiln ❺, and shortly

beyond that the route returns to the woodland paths. There is a brief, open section where the path passes between dense gorse thickets and here the view opens out to show Neath and the river valley. Once into the woods, the narrow path runs under the shadow of tall, rocky outcrops and along the way the hillside has been eaten into by quarries. The path reaches the perimeter fence of the Wild Life Park by a twisting alpine slide, like a mini Cresta run, before rejoining the path from Aberdulais that leads back to the start of the walk.

▶ *The steps, railings and seats to be found in the woods around Aberdulais are all made from home-grown logs.*

Industrial Landscape

The Falls became famous as a beauty spot in the 18th century, when the cult of the picturesque was at its height. At that time a new taste was developed for wild, romantic scenery and the falls perfectly fitted into the tourists' notion of the ideal landscape. It is easy to see how the scene appealed to such famous artists as Turner and Ruskin. The River Dulais crashes down in spectacular fashion, and the falls themselves are overhung by tall, rocky crags. But by 1861, when Mr and Mrs S. C. Hall came to see the falls and write their book on South Wales, they reported that 'the tourist need not pause to visit them now, for the iron lords have ruined their picturesque'. In fact, industry had arrived here long before the 19th century, and the appeal of the site today depends as much on its industrial history as its natural beauty.

The story of the area's industrial development really begins across the Bristol Channel in Cornwall and Devon, where copper was being mined. In order to obtain the metal from the ore it needs to be smelted, heated in a furnace. Unfortunately, while the south-west of England had the ore, it did not have the fuel, and it proved cheaper to export the copper than to bring in the fuel. There was, however, both fuel and water to turn wheels to provide power in South Wales. In the 1580s Queen Elizabeth I paid for a German expert to come over to Aberdulais to establish a copper smelter by the falls. It was a great success, and soon nearby Swansea became the centre of a vast copper smelting industry and remote Aberdulais went into decline.

Neath then developed as an iron working site, and Aberdulais was converted to an iron works in 1667. This too failed. The arrangements that were made to use water power on the site were not wasted, however, and a grain mill was established. When the mill complex was demolished, iron working briefly returned to Aberdulais, to be followed by the final industrial phase when tin-plating was introduced and continued nearly to the end of the 19th century.

The Victorian bastion and waterwheel pit (above) of the tin-plate period are a reminder of the long and varied industrial history at Aberdulais Falls. They are now undergoing extensive restoration work. Looking back to an industrious past — Aberdulais Mill (right) was painted by J. M. W. Turner in around 1796.

◄ *The view west from Overton Cliff along the rugged coastline. Tree mallow (inset), which can grow to 10 feet (3m), is a rare plant found only in Wales and Cornwall. It can be seen on the walk.*

Inside, there are some stone shelves along the walls. These niches may have been nesting holes for pigeons; some people think this intriguing structure was a dovecote for the now-vanished Port-Eynon Castle, since a similar structure has survived at nearby Oxwich Castle. Others maintain that Culver Hole was a smugglers' den.

SECRET PASSAGEWAY

Yet another theory suggests that it was a Celtic hermit's retreat, dating from the 6th century. John Lucas of the Salt House is reported to have rebuilt 'Kulverd Hall' in the 16th century and used it as a stronghold. This has given rise to the fanciful legend of a secret passageway leading to the Salt House through the limestone cliffs.

From above Overton Mere, the clifftop path leads westwards

A smuggling village and ancient caves on the rocky Gower coast

This walk takes in a curved sandy beach and a rocky inlet (both good for swimming), an old fishing village with a smuggling past, intriguing architectural remains, caves once inhabited by prehistoric people and animals, and clifftop farmland.

The route starts from a village with a salty past. Port-Eynon was named after an 11th-century Welsh prince who built a castle here. No trace now remains. Despite the growing demands of recreation and tourism, this seaside village retains much of its ancient character, with narrow lanes and a Norman church.

SMUGGLERS' COAST

The village was once a haven for a rough breed of seaborne adventurers, and in the late 18th century, when smuggling was in its heyday, up to eight Customs and Excise men had to be stationed in the village.

To the south of the village is the Salt House **A**, which consists of the remains of several fishermen's cottages. Visible today are the foundations of two that were occupied until the 1860s. Salt for curing fish was made there by evaporating sea water. The sea reaches the old walls at high water, and at low tide the remains of other structures are visible, including stone vaults that once formed a quay. The original Salt House was a fortified mansion belonging to John Lucas, a 16th-century adventurer.

Further south along the rocky shore, Port-Eynon Point offers a good view back to the curved beach and westwards along the coast. Below the point lie two ridges of sand and rock that can be approached from the shore, but are cut off by spring tides. The easiest to get to is Sedgers Bank, while Skysea lies further from the shore.

A cave lies at the tip of Port-Eynon Point. It can be reached at low tide via a track along the shore from the Salt House. Prehistoric bones have been found inside the cave, but this site does not really compare with other caves further along the walk.

Around the headland are Overton Mere, and Culver Hole **B**, the focus of many local legends. The Hole's outer wall of masonry — built in the narrow cleft between two cliffs that fall steeply to the sea, and pierced with windows — stands 60 feet (18m) high. It is almost impossible to scale without using ladders or climbing gear.

FACT FILE

✴ Port-Eynon, 10 miles (16km) south-west of Swansea, on the A4118

🗺 Pathfinder 1126 (SS 49/59, SS 48/58/68), grid reference SS 468851

| miles 0 | 1 | 2 | 3 | 4 | 5 | 6 | 7 | 8 | 9 | 10 miles |
| kms 0 | 1 2 | 3 | 4 | 5 | 6 | 7 | 8 9 | 10 11 | 12 13 | 14 15 kms |

🕐 4 hours

▬ The basic walk is rocky, but not particularly difficult underfoot. Suggested short diversions involve steep scrambles. Walking boots are recommended. Check tide times before starting the walk

P Car park at the start

T Regular bus service from Swansea

🍴 Pubs, shops and restaurants in Port-Eynon

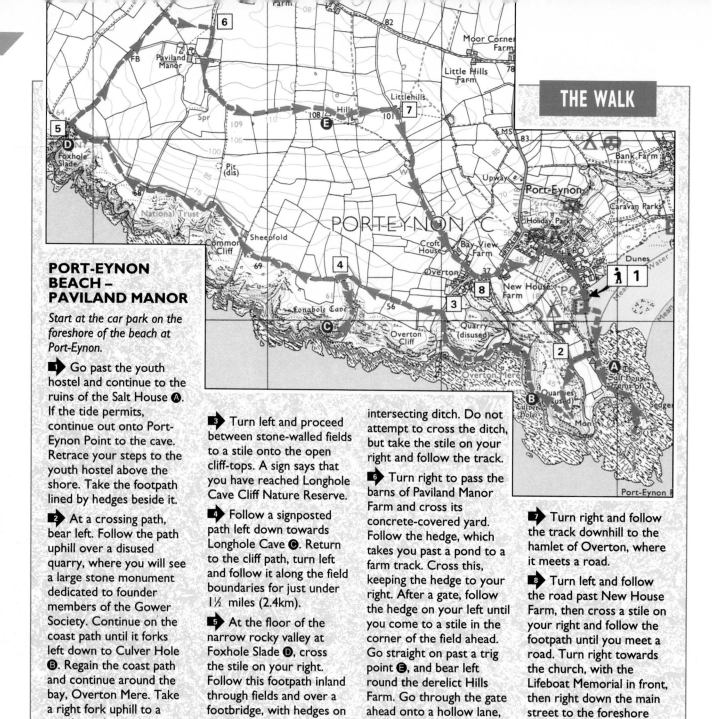

PORT-EYNON BEACH – PAVILAND MANOR

Start at the car park on the foreshore of the beach at Port-Eynon.

▶1 Go past the youth hostel and continue to the ruins of the Salt House **A**. If the tide permits, continue out onto Port-Eynon Point to the cave. Retrace your steps to the youth hostel above the shore. Take the footpath lined by hedges beside it.

▶2 At a crossing path, bear left. Follow the path uphill over a disused quarry, where you will see a large stone monument dedicated to founder members of the Gower Society. Continue on the coast path until it forks left down to Culver Hole **B**. Regain the coast path and continue around the bay, Overton Mere. Take a right fork uphill to a rough road.

▶3 Turn left and proceed between stone-walled fields to a stile onto the open cliff-tops. A sign says that you have reached Longhole Cave Cliff Nature Reserve.

▶4 Follow a signposted path left down towards Longhole Cave **C**. Return to the cliff path, turn left and follow it along the field boundaries for just under 1½ miles (2.4km).

▶5 At the floor of the narrow rocky valley at Foxhole Slade **D**, cross the stile on your right. Follow this footpath inland through fields and over a footbridge, with hedges on your left, until you reach an intersecting ditch. Do not attempt to cross the ditch, but take the stile on your right and follow the track.

▶6 Turn right to pass the barns of Paviland Manor Farm and cross its concrete-covered yard. Follow the hedge, which takes you past a pond to a farm track. Cross this, keeping the hedge to your right. After a gate, follow the hedge on your left until you come to a stile in the corner of the field ahead. Go straight on past a trig point **E**, and bear left round the derelict Hills Farm. Go through the gate ahead onto a hollow lane, down to Littlehills cottage.

▶7 Turn right and follow the track downhill to the hamlet of Overton, where it meets a road.

▶8 Turn left and follow the road past New House Farm, then cross a stile on your right and follow the footpath until you meet a road. Turn right towards the church, with the Lifeboat Memorial in front, then right down the main street to the foreshore and car park.

---

towards three of the most interesting caves in Glamorgan. Longhole Cave **C**, high on Overton Cliff, is about 130 feet (39m) above the high water mark, and is reached by a footpath branching off the main track. Animal remains and prehistoric artefacts have been discovered here by archaeologists; many are now in the British Museum and the National Museum of Wales.

Paviland Caves lie lower down the cliffs near Foxhole Slade **D**. Both are difficult to find and extremely dangerous to approach, due to incoming tides and crumbling cliff paths. The larger cave, Goat's Hole,

▼*The wall across the cleft of Culver Hole may have been part of a dovecote.*

has yielded some of the richest finds in Britain for archaeologists. A headless skeleton stained red was unearthed from its floor in 1823, and by 1913 over 800 implements, along with many Ice Age animal bones, had been uncovered.

FINAL VIEWS

The route back to Port-Eynon follows well-trodden footpaths and quiet byways inland across beautiful farmland. The trig point **E** near Hills Farm offers a fabulous panorama of the South Gower headland on a fine day. From here there is an easy descent to Port-Eynon village.

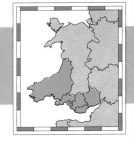

Explore a historic estate set in industrial South Wales

▲ *A modern sculpture, 'First Try' by Gordon Young, in front of Margam Castle. Behind it, to the right, is the site of the Iron Age hill fort. Fallow deer (right) roam the park all year.*

Margam Country Park is sandwiched between the steel works and refineries of Port Talbot, and forested moorland. The coastal plain here is crossed by the M4 and blighted with derelict farms.

Belying its unpromising site, the 800-acre (324-hectare) estate is a splendid concentration of grand buildings, ancient sites and works of art, all set in rolling parkland with mature specimen trees, some rare. There are wild gardens, ponds, streams and a cascade, and walkers can roam at will among herds of deer.

CISTERCIAN FOUNDATION

The walk begins in the oldest building, Margam Abbey Church Ⓐ, the remains of a Cistercian house founded by the son of Henry I in 1147. The Cistercians, a hard-working, reforming order, set up farms and mills and had a great civilizing influence on the area.

The church consists of the restored remains of the abbey's nave. Cistercians rejected ornament in their churches, but there are great riches here. William Morris and Edward Burne-Jones created the

FACT FILE

* Margam Park Country Park, 2 miles (3.2km) south-west of Port Talbot, off the A48

* Pathfinder 1146 (SS 78/88), grid reference SS 801862

miles 0 1 2 3 4 5 6 7 8 9 10 miles
kms 0 1 2 3 4 5 6 7 8 9 10 11 12 13 14 15 kms

* Allow 3 to 4 hours

* Good walking on well maintained paths throughout. The walk is set in a country park, and a charge is payable

P By the Abbey Church at the start

T BR trains to Port Talbot, and an hourly bus service from there to Margam

* Several snack bars and cafés and toilets in the country park

* For opening times of Margam Country Park, Tel. (01639) 881635. For information on the church and Stones Museum, Tel. (01639) 891548

Victorian stained glass in the west windows, and the painted alabaster tombs of the Mansel family are some of the best Tudor and Jacobean monuments anywhere. The Mansels took over the estate when the abbey was dissolved. When their line ran out, it was inherited by the Talbot family, whose memorials are in smooth Italian marble.

The ruins of the abbey, including a twelve-sided chapter house, stand behind the church. Close by is a magnificent lace beech tree, whose branches sweep the ground.

Margam is now owned and maintained by the West Glamorgan Council, and there is a small entrance fee for walkers. Not far from the ticket office is a long, low, Classical building with a row of tall windows. This is the Orangery Ⓑ, built in the 1780s to provide winter

THE WALK

MARGAM COUNTRY PARK

The walk begins by Margam Abbey Church Ⓐ. Follow signs for the country park from junction 38 on the M4, then for the abbey from the A48.

1 Leave via the side door to view the ruins of the Cistercian abbey. This takes you into Margam Country Park. Go straight ahead, through a gate, to the entrance booth.

2 Purchase a walkers' ticket, then retrace your steps to the Orangery Ⓑ and turn left to walk through the gardens. At the far end, turn right to the Temple of the Graces. Turn left to the maze Ⓒ, which can be viewed from a platform.

3 Take the signposted path to the old citrus house and gardening museum, and continue to the ticket office once more. Go through the sculpture park Ⓓ and along the farm trail to the nature reserve. Bear left around the reserve towards New Pond. Go round the pond, keeping the water to your left. Walk straight ahead to Margam Castle Ⓔ.

4 Turn right, downhill, and follow the waymarked path to the hill fort of Mynydd y Castell Ⓕ. Follow the path to the top, then retrace your steps to the embankment and turn left on the path around the fort. Follow this right, then left along the bank of the abbey's fishpond.

5 Take a path sharp right, up to Hen Eglwys Ⓖ.

centuries. The hill fort on Mynydd y Castell Ⓕ was probably built by Celts driven west by the Romans.

Retrace your steps to the valley below the fishpond. Turn right to pick up the minor road signposted to the Abbey Church and Stones Museum Ⓗ, to return to the start.

▲*The 18th-century Orangery, its terrace enlivened by Classical statuary, once housed the estate's citrus trees.*

quarters for the estate's collection of citrus trees. The trees were wheeled out through the high central door to enjoy the summer sunshine.

Nearby is the Temple of Graces, built in Classical style. Four Graces are depicted in the sculpture niches, though three was all the Greeks and Romans ever needed. The nearby 17th-century Summer Banqueting House, now the Citrus House, functions as a gardening museum.

Beyond these buildings is a maze Ⓒ, the largest in Europe. More than 3,000 cypress trees, planted in 1984, enclose a walk over 1 mile (1.6km) long; there are maps available for those who wish to venture in.

From the buildings, the route goes through a sculpture park Ⓓ of contemporary work, and along a farm trail, where there are Vietnamese pot-bellied pigs and red and Père David's deer, as well as fallow deer, which roam all through the park. The route skirts a nature reserve and New Pond, which was built as a boating lake.

FANTASTIC CASTLE

Behind the pond rises Margam Castle Ⓔ, built in the 1830s for Christopher Rice Mansel Talbot, 'Britain's wealthiest commoner' and for 60 years MP for Glamorgan. This 41-bedroom Gothic fantasy needed more than 100 servants to run it, and an enormous tonnage of coal to heat it; fortunately, Mr Talbot was also the owner of the local mines.

The hall and its impressive octagonal tower have been restored and opened to visitors. The view from the crenellated parapets encompasses the vast estate, which stretches down to Port Talbot (the creation of the Talbot family), where Talbot ships were loaded, the houses belched Talbot coal-smoke and the inhabitants drank Talbot ale.

The hills above the castle have ruins that predate it by several centuries. The hill fort on Mynydd y Castell Ⓕ was probably built by Celts driven west by the Romans.

On a spur above the abbey are the romantic ruins of Hen Eglwys Ⓖ. This 15th-century chapel may have been either a private oratory for the later Cistercian abbots or a place of worship for the lay brothers and workers of the abbey.

Near the end of the walk is the Margam Stones Museum Ⓗ. The building, one of the earliest church schools in Britain, now houses a collection of inscribed and sculpted stones, from the Romano-Celtic period up to the Middle Ages, either found on the estate or bought from neighbouring landowners by some members of the Talbot family who were amateur antiquarians.

▼*The attractive New Pond, the largest of the park's waters, was created as a boating and fishing lake for the Talbots.*

FACT FILE

☀ Pembrokeshire National Park, 2 miles (3.2km) west of St David's on the road leading to Porthstinian

▭ Pathfinder 1055 (SM 62/72), grid reference SM 723252

miles 0   1   2   3   4   5   6   7   8   9   10 miles

kms 0 1 2 3 4 5 6 7 8 9 10 11 12 13 14 15 kms

◐ Allow 1½ hours

▬ An easy walk following the coastline. Take special care where the path is close to the edge of the cliffs, especially in strong winds. Do not attempt to cross the sandbar on foot

P Public car park near the ruined chapel of St Justinian

🍴 Restaurants, pubs and shops at St David's

◀ *Dangerous Ramsey Sound can look tranquil on a fine day. (below) Grey seals are found along this coast.*

A coastal walk overlooking Ramsey Sound

This leisurely walk offers something for everyone. The dramatic Pembroke coastline offers breathtaking scenery, and the area is rich in a huge variety of sea birds and wild flowers. The chapel of St Justinian and an ancient earthwork are steeped in local legend. There is also a chance to visit St David's lifeboat station, whose crews have risked their lives saving many others, along this treacherous coast.

The walk begins at St Justinian's Chapel **Ⓐ**. He was a holy man who came from Brittany and established a religious community on Ramsey Island in the 6th century. A faithful companion of St David and, living a

very disciplined but simple life, he expected his followers to do the same. According to local tradition he was murdered on his island by his servants, but he apparently rose to his feet and walked across the Sound, carrying his decapitated head under his arm. He was buried on the spot where his ruined chapel now stands. Originally it was a Celtic foundation but it was rebuilt in about 1510 by Bishop Vaughan.

St David's Lifeboat Station **Ⓑ** was originally established in 1869 on

St David's Lifeboat Station. The lifeboat, Garside, was called out 13 times in 1989 — once in force 11 gales!

the edge of the coast above Porthstinian. The existing building was constructed in 1911 at a cost of £3000. Since that time its crews have participated in numerous rescues along this very dangerous stretch of coastline. For opening times of the station, Tel. (01437) 720392. The cliff scenery on this headland is particularly spectacular and across the water can be seen Ramsey Island **Ⓒ**. It is separated from the mainland by a narrow and dangerous tide race which runs at up to 10 knots at times. Sunken rocks make navigation extremely dangerous.

BIRD SANCTUARY

Ramsey Island or Ynys Tyfanog (Tyfanog's Island), to use its old Welsh name, is 2 miles (3.2 km) long, 1 mile (1.6 km) wide and extends over 600 acres (243 hectares). It has two heather-clad hills of igneous rock which are called Carn Llundain, 443 feet (135 metres), and Carn Ysgubor, 328 feet (100 metres), and they both have Bronze Age cairns on their summits. A survey undertaken on the island in 1326 recorded that it could support 10 horses, 100 cattle and 300 sheep and produce 500 rabbits a year. It was farmed until 1968 but now it is a bird reserve popular with choughs and is a nesting ground for large colonies of kittiwakes, guillemots and razorbills.

On nearing Rhosson Farm, the rocky hill of Clegyr Boia can be

THE WALK

PEMBROKESHIRE COASTAL PATH

From St David's follow the road west to Porthstinian. There is a public car park just before the end of the road, near the ruined chapel of St Justinian **A**.

1 From the car park follow the coastal footpath to the right, passing above

bird sanctuary, Ramsey Island **C**.

2 The well-trodden path leads around the headland, passing above the inlet of Porth Cadnaw. In places there is a dramatic drop on the seaward side so take particular care if you are accompanied by young children.

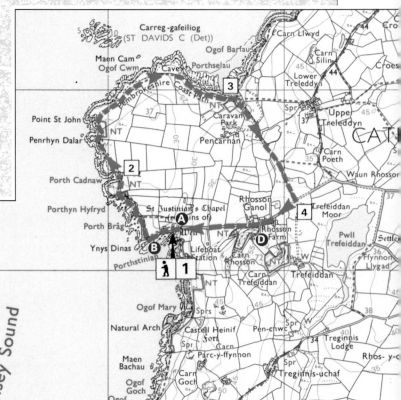

the St David's Lifeboat Station **B**. Hugging the edge of the headland, this path gives a view of some very spectacular coastal scenery, and across the sound is the

3 On reaching the sandy bay of Porthselau, turn right and follow a path beside a stream, which tumbles down to enter the sea. Ignore a footpath sign pointing left

and keep straight on. Turn right at the next junction to follow a cart track.

4 Turn right where the track meets a road. Across to the left can be seen an

ancient fortified site known as Clegyr Boia. Soon on the left you will pass Rhosson Farm **D**. Follow the road back to the car park, near the chapel, at the start.

◄ *The ruins of St Justinian's chapel.*
► *Visitors can make boat trips to tiny Ramsey Island to see the many sea birds whose sole preserve it now is.*

seen. The earthwork crowning it was once occupied by an Irish chieftain, Boia, who caused problems for St David when he tried to establish his Christian community. Eventually the troublesome Irishman was destroyed, either by a bolt of lightning (as legend has it) or at the hands of an Irish pirate.

Rhosson Farm **D** is an old farmhouse with an unusual, large, round

'Flemish' chimney, which has become a local landmark. It was here that the local Pembrokeshire historian Richard Fenton was born. In the early part of the 19th century, he published his *Historical Tour Through Pembrokeshire*.

If you follow this walk in the summer you will be delighted by a wide variety of wild flowers, which may include thrift, pennywort, sea campion, violets, white daisies and clusters of beautiful, yellow primroses. The hedges are ablaze with golden gorse and the sea pinks rustle like paper in the breeze. May and

June are the best months for seeing the flowers in full bloom.

Atlantic grey seals may be seen fishing in Ramsey Sound, and between September and November they come ashore to breed.

◄ The view from the top of Constitution Hill is spectacular on a clear day. Sea campion (inset) is common on the cliff tops.

octagonal tower in which the admission charge brings you the services of a 14-inch (35-cm) lens system to focus detailed views on a screen in a darkened viewing gallery.

DYFED

IRON AGE HILLFORT

After Penglais Woods, there is a view across Aberystwyth. From here you can also see the monument on the top of Pen Dinas, the Iron Age hillfort south of the town. This is shaped like a canon barrel and was erected in 1852 in memory of the Duke of Wellington.

The buildings of the university at the top of the hill on your left are a reminder of the 100,000 or more small donations, from coal mines and chapels, that paid for the establishment of this seat of learning. Part of it is still located in the hotel on the sea front, which was bought at a bargain price from a speculator and became the University College of Aberystwyth in 1872.

One of its most notable students was Prince Charles who came here to study Welsh in 1969 before his

A walk along the cliff tops then through woods above Aberystwyth

Choose a clear day to enjoy the views from the cliff-top path and Aberystwyth on the way back. There is a stiff climb up Constitution Hill, but you could avoid this by taking the Cliff Railway.

The view from the top extends from Strumble Head in the south to Bardsey Island, off the tip of the Lleyn Peninsula, in the north. After overlooking the valley of the River Clarach, you return through attractive oak woodland.

The Tourist Information Centre is next to the Ceredigion Museum **Ⓐ**, which is housed in the restored Edwardian Coliseum Theatre.

Having walked past the beach you may be tempted by the Cliff Railway **Ⓑ** up Constitution Hill. A small fee will save you the 400-foot (120-metre) climb if you go between 10am and 6pm from Easter to October. The longest electric cliff railway in Great Britain, it leads to the Camera Obscura **Ⓒ**. This is an

FACT FILE

⚹ Aberystwyth, Dyfed

⌖ Pathfinder 926 (SN57/58), grid reference SN 583818

miles 0   1   2   3   4   5   6   7   8   9   10 miles
kms 0   1   2   3   4   5   6   7   8   9   10   11   12   13   14   15 kms

◕ Allow 2½ hours

▭ Easy, except for the steep climb up Constitution Hill, which can be avoided by taking the Cliff Railway in season. Good walking shoes are highly recommended

P Car park opposite the Tourist Information Centre near the sea front in the centre of the town (signposted)

T Trains and buses to the station, from where you take Ffordd y Mor (Terrace Road) towards the sea

WC Toilets and refreshments in Aberystwyth and at the top of Constitution Hill (in season)

►Aberystwyth's electric cliff railway is the longest in the country and saves the steep climb up Constitution Hill.

THE WALK

ABOVE ABERYSTWYTH

The walk begins at the Tourist Information Centre **A** *at the corner of Ffordd y Mor (Terrace Road) and Bath Street, Aberystwyth. There is a car park facing it, while the railway station and bus stops are at the other end of Ffordd y Mor.*

1 Go along Ffordd y Mor towards the sea. Turn right along Marine Terrace (becoming Victoria Terrace) to walk with the sea on your left. Go right at the end, towards the Cliff Railway **B**.

2 Just before the Cliff Railway, go left along the zigzag path up Constitution Hill. This is fairly steep but there are benches. Go right over a footbridge across the railway, then left to re-cross it by a second bridge. Reach a café and the Camera Obscura **C** at the top.

3 Go towards the sea and turn right along the cliff-top path (not the broader path inland of it). Walk with a fence on your right and below a radar station.

4 Just before the coastal path goes ahead through conifer trees, turn right over a stile and bear left above the trees. Cross a stile beside a gate on your left to descend along a path

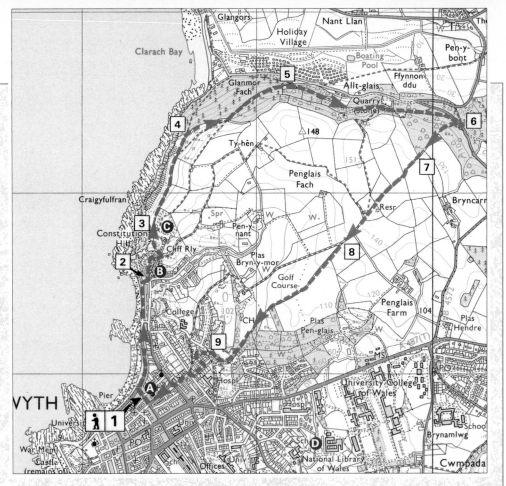

through the conifers.

5 Emerge at a hairpin bend in a lane above a caravan site. Fork right uphill to pass a cottage on your right. When the lane bends sharply right uphill, take the waymarked path through the broad-leaved trees ahead. Ignore a path on your right, go ahead to a waymark post and fork left. Pass old stone quarries on your right, ignore a path which forks steeply downhill on your left and go ahead along a path which very gradually descends to a road.

6 Just before the road go sharply right, up a path

through the trees. Continue with a hedge on your left and trees on your right to a kissing gate.

7 Go ahead through the kissing gate and with a fence on your left. Cross a stile to the left of a field gate ahead and walk with a fence on your right to a stile ahead. Cross this and veer slightly left across a field between two ruins to a waymarked stile. Go ahead along a fenced track. Ignore the hedged track on your left.

8 Bear left at a fork. Walk with a hedge on your left and a golf course on your right. Pass picnic

tables in woodland on your left. You can then stop to admire the view across Aberystwyth to the National Library of Wales **D**. Go ahead down steps and bear right to the road.

9 Go left, then right and left downhill on the road to a junction. Go right down Trefor Road, turn right at North Road, then left down Loveden Road. Veer right across Queen's Road to go up Stryd Portland (Portland Street). This leads to Ffordd y Mor. You can now go right, back to the car park at the start of the walk, or left, to the station and bus stop.

investiture as Prince of Wales. The most eye-catching building is the National Library of Wales **D**. An Englishman, Stuart Rendel, gave the land for it in 1897. This splendid building houses millions of books, maps, pictures and manuscripts, including the 12th-century Welsh *Black Book of Carmarthen*.

A trip to Aberystwyth would not be complete without a ride on the Vale of Rheidol Narrow Gauge

▶ *The coastal path runs along the cliffs between Aberystwyth and Clarach Bay.*

Steam Railway. Opened in 1902 to serve the lead mines, it runs inland for nearly 12 miles (19.2 km) at a gradient of 1:48 to Devil's Bridge. Trains run from the station. This is also the terminus of the standard gauge line from Shrewsbury. The building also houses the Aberystwyth Yesterday Exhibition.

A walk from historic castle sites overlooking a once-bustling river

▲The silting up of the Teifi Estuary put an end to Cardigan's future as a major port. The bar-tailed godwit (below), a winter visitor, was regarded by the Anglo-Saxons as a tasty delicacy.

Cardigan is known as Aberteifi in Welsh, meaning the mouth of the Teifi. Its English name reflects that it was the country town of Cardiganshire, now swallowed up in Dyfed. Cardigan is a corruption of Ceredigion, the land of Ceredig. He was a son of Cunedda, who was responsible for re-asserting British rule in north and west Wales in the 5th century, when the area appeared likely to become an Irish colony.

A bustling little market town today, Cardigan was once a major port. Warehouses crowded around the bridge, which dates from 1726. Herring was an important product, with vast quantities of salt brought here from Liverpool in order to preserve the fish. Ships also came with seed-corn, tallow and limestone. Leaving the port would be slate from Cilgerran (just upstream), ale from Cardigan and local salmon and oak. Inns added to the exotic flavour, some being notorious for prostitutes and cutpurses.

Ships were built here until 1877 and 292 vessels, with a total weight of about 10,000 tons, were registered here in the 1820s. Most of the ships

THE WALK

CARDIGAN

The walk starts from the Cardigan side of the bridge.

▶ Face the walls of Cardigan Castle Ⓐ and bear left up Bridge Street and into the High Street. Opposite the Black Lion Hotel, turn left to follow Ebens Lane (at the corner of which is the Midland Bank). At the end of the lane, go right and almost immediately left to cross a footbridge over a stream.

2 Go left along a path which overlooks a car park. Continue past a cemetery on your right. Follow a roughly metalled track above the River Teifi on your left and past a children's playground on your right. Reach the entrance to a sewage works and take the narrow path on its left, overlooking the river Ⓑ. Go ahead through a kissing gate.

3 Turn right over a waymarked stile in the fence on your right. Follow a hedge on your left towards a gate ahead, but veer right as you approach it to cross a stile in the hedge facing you. Turn right along the hedged Old Castle Road. The name Old Castle refers to the site Ⓒ on your left beyond Old Castle Farm. Follow the road to a T-junction.

4 Turn left to follow a lane with a strip of grass down its centre. Go left around a bend towards the Teifi Estuary, then bend right with the lane towards the sea. When the lane veers left, go straight ahead as signposted, through a kissing gate beside a field gate to enter a field at a corner. Walk with a hedge on your left and go ahead through three more kissing gates between fields.

5 Go ahead over a waymarked stile and with the estuary on your left. Continue through a waymarked kissing gate to take a path down to a beach Ⓓ. Maintain your direction to a road and turn right along it for 100 yards (90 metres).

6 Turn left down a private drive and bear right immediately towards a house. At the house, turn left over a bridge and through a gate, then over a stile in the hedge facing you. Pass farm buildings on left and go ahead over a stile beside a gate. Bear right to follow a track with a hedge on your right. Pass wild hops and apple trees Ⓔ on left, carry on above a farm on your right then descend to its access track. Bear left along it. Fork right along a lane.

7 Turn right at a T-junction to follow a road to another T-junction. Turn right and reach the B4548.

8 Turn left along the B4548 for 15 yards (13.5 metres) then turn right across it, as signposted, to follow an access lane for 300 yards (279 metres). Go straight ahead through a kissing gate when the lane bends right. Walk with a hedge on your left and over two stiles beside gates ahead to go through a kissing gate beside a field gate next to a signpost and rejoin your outward lane. Turn left along it. Go past Old Castle Road on right.

9 Take the next turning on your right. Pass the cemetery on your right and turn left to retrace your steps over the footbridge and back to the start.

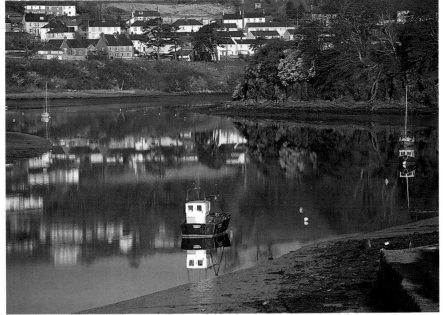

were share-owned by local farmers. Many emigrants left here for New Brunswick in Canada, or for New York. The railway finally came to Cardigan on the opposite bank of the Teifi in 1885. Its arrival and the silting up of the river hastened the decline of the port and the town was forced to seek a new future as a base for fishing and touring holidays.

ABBEY RUINS

The picturesque view across the River Teifi **B** includes St Dogmaels. The remains of the old abbey here, established by the Welsh in the 7th century, are well worth exploring. The abbey was sacked by the Vikings, rebuilt by the Normans in

▼*Cardigan Bridge leads across the River Teifi to a wildlife park, which is home to a wide variety of animals and birds typical of this area of Wales.*

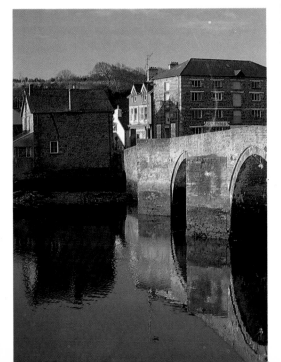

▲*Small fishing boats are a common sight in the Teifi Estuary. St Dogmaels (below), across the river from Cardigan, is the start of the 168-mile (270-km) long Pembrokeshire Coast Path.*

Montgomery, swept across Wales in 1093, they erected a small castle here. This simple motte and bailey structure was soon dismantled by the Welsh. There is a record of a Din Geraint being built near the estuary of the Teifi by Gilbert FitzRichard in 1110, when Henry I dispossessed the Welsh lord Cadwgan of his lands.

CASTLE ORIGINS

The bridge over the Teifi is over-looked by Cardigan Castle **A**, which is of historical interest, especially to lovers of Welsh culture. Whether or not the Din Geraint of 1110 was built here or downstream, there was a castle on this spot in 1136. The Welsh had still not been conquered, so they gathered to deal with the affront of a Norman castle in their midst. The Normans, led by William and Maurice, two sons of Gerald of Windsor, led their men out of the

the 12th century and finally fell into ruin during Tudor times. The parish church contains an old ogham stone and the watermill still produces wholemeal flour. St Dogmaels still has a fishing industry based on sea trout, or sewin as they are called in Wales, and salmon, now mainly centred on the River Teifi.

On this side of the river is Old Castle Farm, in whose private grounds is the site of Din Geraint **C**, an Iron Age fort. When the Normans, under Roger de

castle to fight the Welsh at a place called Crug Mawr. They were defeated and the English colony around the castle was set on fire. The Normans fled across the bridge back to their castle, but the weight of horses and armoured men broke it and the river was full of bodies. The castle survived and was not taken by the Welsh until Rhys ap Gruffydd, the great Lord Rhys, drove the Normans out in 1164.

The Teifi soon flows into a broad estuary bounded by saltmarsh and dunes ⓓ. The continual movement of underwater sandbanks made the mouth of the estuary a problem for sailors to negotiate. Waders positively love the mudflats, however, while other birds abound. Abandoned smallholdings would appear to account for the aroma of apples and hops as you walk along the attractive track ⓔ between Aberdare and Felin Bedr.

Further along the estuary and less than ¼ mile (400 metres) offshore lies Cardigan Island, a nature reserve

▲The aroma of hops and apples from abandoned smallholdings fills the air along the field track. The remains of Din Geraint, an Iron Age hill fort and later a Norman castle, are sited in the grounds of Old Castle Farm (below).

Cardigan Castle

Rhys ap Gruffydd celebrated his triumph over the Normans by building a new stone castle in 1171. Five years later, in 1176, he made it the venue of the earliest recorded eisteddfod. This had been planned for over a year, with proclamations all over the British Isles. Competitions were held for two chairs. One, confined to Welsh-speakers, was to find the best bard. The other, open to members of any nation, was for the best musician, playing an instrument of their choice. The chief bard had long been awarded 'the chair' after a competition at an eisteddfod, but Lord Rhys held the first that had a written record. The present Royal National Eisteddfod descends from this tradition and this annual highlight of the Welsh year (covering the first full week in August at a different location alternating between North and South Wales) was held in Cardigan in 1976, on the 800th anniversary of Lord Rhys. As now, the best music was made in South Wales, while the best poetry came from the North.

The usual Celtic failing of fighting amongst themselves was to follow Rhys' death in 1197. One of Rhys'

sons, Maelgwn, betrayed his brother Gruffudd to the Normans. King John recognized him as paying homage for Ceredigion, in return for the gift of Cardigan Castle. 'Maelgwn ap Rhys sold to the Saxon the lock and stay of all Wales, the castle of Cardigan, for a small worthless price.' It assumed great importance in the late 13th century as the English finally conquered Wales. It even withstood Owain Glyndwr until 1405. Lasting damage was effected during the Civil War, however. The present walls were largely rebuilt in the 18th century.

The south-east tower is basically medieval, as is the east tower, while the north-east bastion is also mostly medieval. Castle Green House was built in 1828 and is haunted by the ghost of Lady Helen Lethbridge, one of its first occupants. She died lonely and miserable after an unhappy marriage. Another ghost is that of a suicide, George Davies. There are also two secret tunnels. One is said to go to St Dogmaels Abbey, while the other goes to Cilgerran.

Largely destroyed during the Civil Wars, Cardigan Castle is now privately owned and only the walls are visible to the public.

belonging to the Dyfed Wildlife Trust and currently the site of a recolonization experiment.

In 1934, a ship being towed to a scrapyard snapped its line in a storm and was wrecked on this tiny isle. The four crew scrambled ashore to safety and, true to form, so did the rats. At the time there was a puffin colony on the island but by the 1940s the birds had left. Their eggs, which are laid in burrows, had fallen prey to the voracious appetite of the invading rats.

In an attempt to attract puffins back to the island, life-size puffins, made of polymer concrete and painted by local schoolchildren, have been placed strategically, in the hope that passing puffins seeking to establish their own breeding territory will land and set up a new colony.

A walk through a National Nature Reserve, past a petrified forest

This is a flat, easy walk with magnificent views of the mountains of Meirionnydd across the Dyfi estuary. There is much to see along the way at close quarters. Nature and legend mingle to make this a very special place. Embankment paths take you over a peat bog before you turn back along a sandy beach to the dunes of Ynyslas, where the Information Centre provides abundant literature on the various forms of wildlife to be seen in the area.

NATURE RESERVE

Admission is free (except for cars) to the National Nature Reserve **A**, which was established at Ynyslas in 1969. The sand dunes here have been formed in the last 400 years by wind-blown sand. The ecological system is very fragile, so avoid damaging it by leaving paths. In the mid-19th century, plans to build a railway bridge across the Dyfi estuary from here were abandoned due to the lack of firm foundations.

The vast expanse of sand on the inland side of the dunes, looking up the Dyfi estuary, is known as Traeth Maelgwyn **B**. It earned its name in

FACT FILE

- Ynyslas, 2 miles (3 km) north of Borth

- Outdoor Leisure Map 23, grid reference SN 610940

  miles 0 1 2 3 4 5 6 7 8 9 10 miles
  kms 0 1 2 3 4 5 6 7 8 9 10 11 12 13 14 15 kms

- Allow 2½ hours

- Over grassy tracks, embankment paths and beach

- [P] At the National Nature Reserve, Ynyslas, at the end of the access lane going north from Ynyslas Turn

- [T] British Rail trains serve Borth (Aberystwyth-Shrewsbury line); Crosville buses nos 511, 512, 520 and 524 from Aberystwyth serve Ynyslas Turn

- [WC] In the Information Centre in Ynyslas National Nature Reserve at start of walk

▲The sand dunes at Ynyslas, now part of a National Nature Reserve, were formed by winds over hundreds of years. Washed up on the beach is Britain's largest jellyfish, the **Rhizostoma octopus** (inset). It is harmless to humans. The view towards Ynyslas, from the river embankment (below).

THE WALK

YNYSLAS

The walk begins at the car park of the National Nature Reserve Ⓐ at Ynyslas. There is a small parking fee, but admission is free.

1 Walk back along the access lane towards Ynyslas Turn. Pass Searivers Caravan Park on your left and a golf course on your right. Reach bungalows on your left and look for a concrete access drive between 'Brynhyfryd' and 'Fairways'. This is opposite a gate on your right. Note view across to the Dyfi estuary and Traeth Maelgwyn Ⓑ.

2 Turn left between the two bungalows. Continue through a gate and straight ahead along a grassy track through two more gates. Maintain your direction along the access drive of a farm on your right to reach a road ahead. Cross the bridge over the Afon Leri Ⓒ.

3 Turn right over a signposted wooden stile to follow a path along the

embankment above the river on your right. Reach the railway and turn right across the railway bridge before crossing the line with care.

4 Walk along the embankment with the river now on your left. Continue over three stiles and notice the former course of the river through the peat bog to Aberlerry Ⓓ on your right.

5 Turn right along a causeway over the bog. Go ahead through a gate and across the railway again. Continue across a golf course to a road. Cross the road and reach the beach.

6 Turn right to walk along the beach with the sea on your left. Look for the petrified forest Ⓔ which is exposed at low tide, then continue to the National Nature Reserve. (Note: the currents make bathing in the sea dangerous here.) Go back to the car park over the sand dunes on the right.

---

the 6th century, when Maelgwn Gwynedd (the Sir Lancelot of the Arthurian tales) held a meeting of the Welsh princes here to determine their overall leader. It was decided to test the contenders with a competition — the winner would be the one able to sit in his chair longest as the tide came in on this beach.

Maeldaf Hen, Maelgwn's adviser, enabled his prince to win by constructing a chair out of waxed birds' wings. The ceremony is re-enacted every year in the Borth Carnival at the end of September.

The Afon Leri Ⓒ is a river that has been turned into a canal. It was redirected towards the estuary in 1824

so that a wharf could be built to take advantage of sheltered moorings. Old ships were sunk to provide a base for the new channel through the peat bogs of Cors Fochno. The river formerly flowed into the sea at Aberlerry Ⓓ.

PETRIFIED FOREST

If you come when the low spring tide is out, you will be transported into another world as you walk along the beach, for you should then see the remains of a petrified forest Ⓔ, including stumps of Scots pine, birch, alder, oak and willow. Legend has an explanation — describing the lost land of Cantre'r Gwaelod, which was drowned by the sea in the 6th century. Its lord, Gwyddno Garanhir, ended up as a fisherman here. Scientists date the forest to about 3,500 BC.

◀ *Borth beach at high tide. When the sea retreats during low spring tides (consult tide tables), you may spot the remains of an old petrified forest — stumps of Scots pine, birch, oak and willow.*

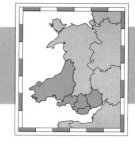
A walk along a coast famed for its wildlife and adventures

The Pembrokeshire coast is renowned for its plant life. In May or June, the coastline is bright with colour and, even in January, there may be up to 50 species in bloom. Buzzards and kestrels are common sights, while the sheltered woodland provides cover for warblers, blackcap and chiffchaff.

This walk out to Carregwastad Point includes a stretch of wild and treacherous coastline, the site of many shipwrecks and a French invasion. Harbour Village was built at the beginning of the 20th century to house railway and port workers

FACT FILE

✳ Goodwick, 1 mile (1.6 km) from Fishguard

🚉 Pathfinder 1032 (SM 83/93), grid reference SM 949390

miles 0　1　2　3　4　5　6　7　8　9　10 miles
kms 0　1　2　3　4　5　6　7　8　9　10　11　12　13　14　15 kms

🕐 Allow 3 hours, plus 15 minutes for diversion

◣ Fairly strenuous in places along the coastal path. Several steep slopes may be slippery in wet weather. Keep well away from the dangerous cliff edges. Good, waterproof walking shoes are essential. Unsuitable for children under eight

🅿 At top of New Road, Harbour Village, Goodwick

🍴 All facilities in Fishguard

Ⓣ British Rail boat trains serve Fishguard, as do boats from Rosslare in Eire. The no. 410 bus from Fishguard terminates at start of walk. Fishguard is also served by no. 411 from St David's and no. 412 from Haverfordwest and Cardigan

▲ *The bay of Aber Felin. Carregwastad Point, where French invaders landed in 1797, is to the north. When the French ships returned to Brest (right) they were attacked by British vessels blockading the port and surrendered.*

and, had things gone according to plan, the harbour ❶ would have become full of transatlantic liners.

An incredible 2,000,000 tons (1,960,000 tonnes) of rock were blasted from the cliffs at Goodwick to be used in the 2,000-foot (610-metre) North Breakwater. The quarry floor became the railway terminus in 1906 and the port opened soon after for transatlantic liners. The ill-judged building of the East Breakwater was to bring an end to the whole scheme in 1913. It caused silting so that the bigger ships were unable to dock.

Many vessels have foundered in these treacherous waters, and the first record of the lifeboat station ❷ dates from 1822. Needle Rock is the last resting place of the Dutch motor schooner *Hermina* which foundered in December 1920. The wreck of the coaster *Gramsbergen* lies east of Needle Rock, where it sank in November 1954.

FRENCH INVASION

From here, the walk continues to Pen Anglas ❸, the Welsh version of the Giant's Causeway in Northern Ireland. The route follows the coastline as far as the memorial ❹ on Carregwastad Point, erected in 1897 to mark the centenary of an attempt-

THE WALK

GOODWICK – CARREGWASTAD POINT – GOODWICK

The walk begins from a small car park at the northern end of the Harbour Village, Goodwick. This is also the bus terminus.

1 With the sea on your right, go ahead along the Pembrokeshire Coast Path. There are fine views of the harbour **A** and the lifeboat station **B** below on your right, as well as across Fishguard Bay to Needle Rock and the site of the wrecked *Gramsbergen*. Walk with a fence on your left at first, then follow the path through bracken after you pass the North Breakwater on your right. Cross a stile and take a wide path with walls broken and obscured by gorse and brambles.

2 Ignore a narrow, walled path going inland on your left. Go towards the sea beside a wall on your right until a waymark post directs you left, with a wall on your left. Go ahead over a stile in the corner. Notice Pen Anglas **C** on your right as you veer right with a wall on your left.

3 Go ahead over a stile in the corner. Turn right between a fence on your left and a wall on your right. Continue over two more stiles to reach a fourth near a signpost. Go ahead along the Coast Path, climbing up to a stile.

Cross it to follow a fence on your left before swinging right with the path between gorse.

4 Descend to cross a stile in the corner and follow a fence on your left. Cross two tiny footbridges over brooks before a third across a stream. Take the stile immediately after it. Go right down a fenced path before bearing left up a steep hill with a wall on your right. Continue along a fenced, grassy clifftop path to the bay of Aber Fellin.

5 Cross a stile ahead and bear right around the bottom of a field. Continue over a second stile with a fence on your left. Turn inland to cross another stile and come to a signpost. You will return here after going out to Carregwastad Point.

6 Take care to remember your next few hundred paces as you will retrace them! Begin by taking the Coast Path down to a stile leading to a footbridge in the wooded valley. Continue up a steep slope to a signpost. Turn

right until you reach a stile in the fence on your right, near another signpost. Take this to follow a path to the memorial **D**.

7 Retrace your steps, remembering to turn left after the second signpost. Climb back up to Stage 6 and proceed directly up hill — do not follow the signpost that points up a small valley. Bear left to a waymark post at the corner of a field. Turn right to follow the fence on your left to a waymarked gate. Go through it and across the centre of the field to a second gate.

8 Take an old green lane ahead to a crosstracks. Go ahead through waymarked gate and follow the left-hand edge of a field to another waymarked gate. Go ahead along a track which is now signposted to a stile. Turn left over this to reach Llanwnda, with its

church **E** on your left.

9 Take the road ahead, forking left before Garnwnda **F**. Pass a cemetery on your right.

10 Go straight ahead at a crossroads to take a farm lane. Pass the access track to Anfield Antiques on your right, then bear right to pass the house on your right. Continue along the green lane, which soon bends left.

11 Go through Pen-rhiw farmyard and take the access track, which starts as a concrete lane.

12 Veer right above Goodwick. Join the road in Harbour Village and turn left along its pavement back to the car park and bus terminus.

ed invasion by the French in 1797. The French believed that the peasants of the United Kingdom were ready to rise up against the crown and sent four ships to help them. They disembarked at Carregwastad Point on the night of 22nd February 1797. Next morning they command-

ed the heights of Garnwnda **F** but were soon overpowered.

After this you turn inland, passing through the ancient settlement of Llanwnda. St Gwyndaf's church **E** is named after a Celtic saint from Brittany. It has a typically Celtic bellcote tower.

To the south of Llanwnda can be seen the craggy volcanic outcrop of Garnwnda, the site of a Neolithic burial chamber. Its capstone is 11 feet (3.4 metres) long by 10½ feet (3.2 metres) wide. A small urn containing calcified bones was found here around 1900.

Nature Walk

The headlands of Britain's rugged coastline are a tough environment for plants and wildlife. Look out for:

STACKS Solitary rock columns standing in the midst of the sea; they were probably once part of the arched entrance to a cave.

SEASHORE LICHENS Bands of coloured lichen line the cliff face from the tide-mark up through the splash zone on hard rock.

FORTIFICATIONS Protected on three sides by the sea, many headlands bear the remains of ancient castles or abandoned fortifications.

CLIFF HEIGHT Gently sloping headlands indicate a sandy substratum; sheer headlands appear in areas of chalk or hard rock.

of this route, including the lighthouse ⊕, from here. The treeless, windswept nature of the landscape enhances its ruggedness. The rock-strewn summit of Garn Fawr bears the remains of an Iron Age fort. The memorial stone ⊕ is for the poet Dewi Emrys (1879–1952).

COASTAL MOUNTAIN

The Pembrokeshire Coast Path ⊕ was officially opened on 16th May, 1970, by Wynford Vaughan Thomas, the broadcaster, who was then president of the Council for the Protection of Rural Wales. It runs for 168 miles (270 km) between Poppit Sands and Amroth. Walking the route is no easy feat — it has been calculated that the total amount of climbing involved is greater than the height of Mount Everest. Now a National Trail, the route is famous for its wildlife — in particular its flowers and birds.

The short diversion to Dinas Mawr ⊕ brings you to the site of an Iron Age promontory fort, perhaps dating from 100 BC. The old Ministry of Defence buildings ⊕ near Pen Brush may provide useful shelter, as well as being landmarks. Pwll Arian ⊕ means Silver Cove or Treasure Cove. This is a delightful spot, where a small valley runs

▶ *During World War I, this compass was carved into the rocks on the top of Garn Fawr. From here, the views across to the headlands are spectacular. A contrast is provided by the view inland from the path beneath Garn Fawr (below).*

down to the sea. The turf is springy and there are plenty of reed beds and copses of bushes.

The lighthouse stands trim and white on the island of Ynys Meicel. It is sometimes accessible by a footbridge, but it is not manned or open to the public. It cost £40,000 to erect in 1908. Nearby is the Coastguard

◀Seen from the coastal path, which you take from here, the youth hostel lies isolated in a windswept landscape.

▶Looking from Dinas Mawr towards Pen Brush, the many rock formations make the coastline look wild and untamed (right).

Tragic End of a Liberty Ship

The *Dan Beard* ● is one of the shipwrecks lying off Strumble Head, and it can still be seen at low water. It lies beneath a vertical cliff wall, at whose base are two tiny pinnacles. The wreck lies between these, with sections of her foremast and winch parts most easily seen lying amongst the rocks.

The *Dan Beard* was a Liberty Ship, built in California in 1943 at an astounding speed. There was an acute shortage of cargo ships owing to losses from German U-boat action — 150 had been sunk during the first year of the war. If Britain were not to be starved into defeat,

The Iberville *leaves New York. Liberty Ships such as this one were built at remarkable speed to support Britain's war effort.*

urgent replacement was needed.

Henry J Kaiser won the contract to build as many cargo ships as possible at his specially constructed shipyard in Richmond, California, where 60 Liberty Ships were launched within two years.

On one of her frequent Atlantic crossings, the 7,176-ton *Dan Beard* was hit by a torpedo fired from the German submarine *U1202* off Strumble Head on 10th December 1944. The ship broke into two and 29 men lost their lives. The stern section sank in deep water, but the bow section drifted ashore beneath Pwll Deri's sheer cliffs. Some of the crew managed to come ashore in the ship's lifeboats, while the St David's lifeboat rescued 12 men.

Station ●. This overlooks a glorious, wild stretch of the Welsh coast which is savagely impressive during storm conditions.

SHIPWRECKED

Around the other side of Strumble Head, at Pwll Bach ●, lies the wreck of the *Salus*. This 3-masted barquentine of 264 tons was attempting to sail around the head in a force 9 gale on 25th September 1896. The ship was soon driven onto rocks and all the crew were swept away within four minutes, the time it took the rescuers to reach the ship.

Notice the pillow-shaped lava cliffs ●. These are the result of lava cooling rapidly as it was thrown out by volcanoes onto what was the sea bed in the Ordovician period. Carreg Gybi ● is named after St Cybi, a Cornishman who sailed up this coast to Caergybi (Holyhead).

▼*Elegantly poised on the island of Ynys Meicel, the lighthouse overlooks the wild coast at Strumble Head.*

THE GOLDEN ROAD

A prehistoric highway past huge, eerie rocks to a fateful, magical spot

The Preseli Hills are an enchant-ed refuge from modern civilization, an area so special that the Pembrokeshire Coast National Park was extended inland to include it. The ancient hills have been worn down to a broad, undulating expanse. Though forested and densely populated from around 3000 BC to AD 100, they are now

FACT FILE

⚗ The Golden Road, Mynydd Preseli, 10 miles (16km) south of Cardigan

ᴏ̄ꜱ Pathfinder 1033 (SN 03/13), grid reference SN 165331

miles 0 1 2 3 4 5 6 7 8 9 10 miles
kms 0 1 2 3 4 5 6 7 8 9 10 11 12 13 14 15 kms

◐ Allow five hours

▬ Some climbs, soft grassy paths and a minor road. A compass is advisable if there is any risk of low cloud obscuring landmarks

P At start of walk

T Infrequent bus services run by Bws Dyfed to Crymych, 1 mile (1.6 km) east of start point, Tel (01792) 475511

🍴 In Crymych

▲The view from the summit of Foeldrygarn stretches as far as Snowdonia and the Black Mountains. Sneezewort (left) grows wild here, but has also been cultivated in gardens.

uninhabited and the only trees are in conifer plantations. The rest is open, windswept moorland with soft peat that is a joy to walk on.

Despite their timeless, remote air, access to the hills is easy. There are some excellent views and the walk is best done on a clear day; a pair of binoculars will come in useful not only for watching birds but also for picking out standing stones and other local landmarks.

The summit of Foeldrygarn (Three Cairn Hill) Ⓐ beckons you from the beginning of the walk. From here there is a commanding view, including the Black Mountains to the east and extending to

THE WALK

BLAEN LLETHR–DAN-Y-GARN

The walk begins at a parking space across the road from a signposted track just over 1 mile (1.6km) west of Crymych.

1 Cross the road to go up the signposted track to its junction with another track from your right.

2 Turn left over a stile in the corner. Bear right immediately along the moorland path that can be seen climbing to the top of Foeldrygarn **A**. Pause to appreciate the view. Bear left when descending, towards a conifer plantation.

3 Turn right along the Golden Road **B** to pass the conifer plantation on your left. When the rocky outcrops of Carn Menyn **C** come into view, make a detour left to inspect them, then return to the old road.

4 Head roughly west towards the prominent rocks of Carn Bica nearly 1 mile (1.6km) ahead; notice the Warrior Stone **D** on your right. Bedd

▼ *Carn Menyn is where Stonehenge's bluestones are thought to have been quarried in prehistoric times.*

Snowdonia in the north and the Wicklow Hills, across the Irish Sea, to the west. The summit from which this magnificent sweep can be enjoyed has three Bronze Age cairns, which give the hill its name. One large, flat stone is called Bwrdd y Brenin (the King's Table) and is said to conceal a pot of gold.

STONEHENGE

The Golden Road **B** was an early Bronze Age trade route. Its name is a reminder that gold was brought along it from the Wicklow Hills. It was still important as a drove road for Welsh Black cattle in the 19th century. It leads past Carn Menyn **C**, from which most of Stonehenge's

bluestones originate. Similar stones, weighing about 4 tons (4 tonnes) each, still litter the site, as if cut ready for transportation.

There are many curious blocks and slabs of rock poised precariously on top of each other, suggesting animal or bird figures, while the top of the distinctively-shaped Warrior Stone **D** resembles a helmet. These are the work of nature. Frost shattered the bedrock when the ground was frozen solid during the last Ice Age. When the glaciers retreated, these great, tumbled forms were left on the surface.

It has long been a mystery how so many of these stones found their way to Wiltshire, where they form

▲ *The stones at Carn Menyn form natural sculptures. Many see the top of the Warrior Stone as a warrior's helmet.*

road, but before reaching it make a sharp right turn to follow another grassy track. Continue over a roughly metalled farm access track to reach a pair of standing stones, Cerrig Meibion Arthur ⓗ.

▶ **7** Retrace your steps to the junction of tracks and go ahead to the road.

▶ **8** Turn left along the road. When a track forks off to the right, go left with the road, until you reach a T-junction. Gorse Fawr stone circle is just one mile (1.6km) down the road on your right, but the present route goes left to Mynachlog-ddu.

▶ **9** Bear left at the junction in Mynachlog-ddu. Follow this road for over two miles (3.2km) back to where the walk began.

Arthur ⓔ is just below Carn Bica on the brow of the hill ahead. Carn Arthur ⓕ is about 300 yards (270m) downhill to the left.

▶ **5** Return uphill to the old road and turn left (west), following white wooden boundary posts. Carn Sian ⓖ is on your left. Descend to a pass with a distinct path on your right.

▶ **6** Turn left to follow an old track running south above the boggy valley on your right. (This path is not always well-defined.) The track swings left towards a

from the south side of Carn Menyn (maybe a few of them from Carn Ddafad-Las, just to the north). He also asserted that four white-spotted blue rhyolite stones came from Carnalw (to the north of here), and three unspotted blue rhyolite stones came from north Carn Menyn.

PREHISTORIC MOVEMENT

It became fashionable for a while to believe that these stones were erratic blocks, carried to within easy reach of Stonehenge by glaciers. Recently, stones that were apparently lost in transit have been dredged up in the rivers of south Dyfed, suggesting that they were in fact moved there by prehistoric men.

At least five stones of volcanic the inner circle and the inner horseshoe of Stonehenge. When Geoffrey of Monmouth wrote his *History of the Kings of Britain* in the 12th century, he stated that Merlin transported the stones of Stonehenge from Ireland. This is not inconsistent with their origin in this part of Wales, which was considered Irish in Merlin's day: an Irish king ruled it, and an ancient Irish language was spoken here.

In 1923, geologist Dr Herbert Thomas established that 60 spotted dolerite stones came to Stonehenge

▶ *Bedd Arthur, an oval of 15 standing stones, is connected with King Arthur. According to legend, he passed here.*

Leys of the Land

Many researchers into mysteries believe that standing stones, stone circles, burial mounds and other ancient sites, as well as pre-Reformation Christian churches, certain hilltops and other natural features, make up a network of straight lines called 'leys' that criss-cross the surface of the earth. Dowsers claim to be able to dowse (detect and trace out) leys.

The concept was first propounded by Alfred Watkins in the 1920s, after he had noticed alignments of geographical and artificial features in his native Herefordshire. He coined the name because there seemed to be an unusual number of place names ending in '-ley' or '-ly' along them. He believed that leys were ancient trade routes along which salt had been transported, despite the fact

A trig point marks the 1200-foot (363-m) summit of Foeldrygarn, which is said to be a node from which several ley lines emanate.

that many of those he discovered ran straight through natural barriers such as cliffs and lakes. Later commentators associate them with occult earth energies. According to one modern view, they are spirit paths, also known as song paths or fairy paths – tracks along which the souls of the dead can pass.

Foeldrygarn is regarded as a centre from which numerous leys radiate. An especially strong one connects it with the ancient site at Carreg Coetan in Newport by way of a burial chamber at Pentre Ifan. Another goes to Mynydd Carningli (the Mountain of the Angels) and a third runs to the Iron Age hill fort situated at Catel Henllys.

formed by 15 stones. Below it is Carn Arthur **F**, a great bluestone rock balanced on a pile of boulders. Nearby Carn Sian **G** is said to be the site of St Silyn's chapel.

The connection with King Arthur is recorded in the story of *Culhwch and Olwen* in the medieval collection of Welsh tales, *The Mabinogion*. Arthur chased after the Twrch Trwyth from Ireland and caught up with him and his host here. Standing at bay in Cwm Cerwyn Twrch Trwyth slew four of Arthur's champions, and then four more, including Arthur's son Gwydre.

VANDALS

Tradition suggests a second of Arthur's sons was killed, because there are two standing stones in the monument known as Cerrig Meibion Arthur **H**. This is a bleak spot, inspiring thoughts of what might have been if Arthur's sons had not died so young. A recognized heir may have prevented the civil war that allowed the Saxons to shape Britain's destiny.

One of the most convincing theories to explain the legend of Arthur and the Twrch Trwyth is that the boar's head was the emblem of the Vandals. As reinforcement to this idea, the medieval historian, Geoffrey of Monmouth, has Arthur sailing to Ireland to deal with African invaders.

If it is accepted that King Arthur was an authentic 6th-century ruler (the son of Meurig) from Gwent, he could well have fought the Vandals here after they had been expelled from North Africa by the forces of the Byzantine empire.

ash from this magical site were also taken in ancient times to Stonehenge. More recently, in Iron Age times, a hill fort enclosed the summit and an outer enclosure, possibly for cattle, was added.

LEGENDARY KING

In the Dark Ages, King Arthur reputedly rode this way with his knights to fight the Twrch Trwyth (Stinking Boar). A bit further along the path is Bedd Arthur **E**, an oval

▶ *Carn Sian, visible from the north-western point of the walk, may be where St Silyn's chapel was located.*

Through a Regency town to clifftops above Cardigan Bay

The mouth of the River Aeron has seen the growth of a tidy, unspoilt little town. The humble fishing village of Aberaeron was transformed in the early 19th century when it was laid out to a set plan. Before the Methodists protested, the locals were noted for bathing naked in the sea on Saturdays. Now holidaymakers resort to its safe beaches. From 1911 to 1951 (when the line was closed) they could have used the railway, but since then the

20th century has not been allowed to intrude too much on this place.

Alban Square ❷ was completed in 1840 and named after Reverend Thomas Alban Jones, who was bequeathed the estate of Lewis Gwynne of Mynachdy. He put the bequest to good use by laying out a neat, spacious town. The Regency architect John Nash, who lived in the area at the time, is said to have taken an interest in the project.

SMARTLY PAINTED

The builders had to conform to a general policy, with large buildings at the ends and centre of each terrace, to avoid monotony. A terracotta limewash had to be painted on the walls of every dwelling at two-yearly intervals, while pebbles from the beach were used to cobble

▲ *Aberaeron Harbour is a lively port, mainly used by pleasure craft, though it has some working boats. Red valerian (left) is a hardy plant that may be seen growing on the shale sea-cliffs.*

FACT FILE

- ✳ Aberaeron, between Cardigan and Aberystwyth

- 🗺 Pathfinder 967 (SN 46/56), grid reference SN 459628

  miles 0 1 2 3 4 5 6 7 8 9 10 miles
  kms 0 1 2 3 4 5 6 7 8 9 10 11 12 13 14 15 kms

- ◗ Allow 2½ hours

- ▬ Fairly strenuous on the cliffs. Paths may be muddy in places; wear good walking shoes

- P Car parks in Aberaeron

- T Buses from Aberystwyth, Bangor, Cardiff, Cardigan, Carmarthen and Tregaron

- 🍴 Pubs, restaurants, cafés and
- WC toilets in Aberaeron

the pavements. (These can still be seen in Belle Vue, as you walk towards the harbour.)

The harbour ❸ is full of colour. There are some small fishing boats and many yachts. The *Zane Spray*, in which disabled yachtsman Dai Sinnot-Jones made his round-the-world trip, may be among them. Aberaeron became a flourishing port after breakwaters were constructed in 1807 and 1811. Butter, corn, cattle and wool were exported, while lime to dress the fields was a vital import. Local oaks also provided timber for shipbuilding.

COASTAL PATH

The harbour is a popular feeding place for gulls, while cormorants can be seen diving for fish. Small house martins flutter around at low tide to gather mud to build their nests under the eaves of nearby houses. The attractive footpath along the shale cliffs ❹ is part of a coastal path being developed by Ceredigion District Council. In time

THE WALK

ABERAERON

*The walk begins from the bus stops opposite the post office in Alban Square **A**, where the A487 passes through the centre of Aberaeron.*

1 With your back to the football pitch, go right. Pass Market Street (down which is a car park) on your right and go ahead over a bridge. Turn right up Harbour Lane to pass the harbour **B** on your right.

2 Go left when you reach the seafront, putting the sea on your right. Keep it there as you take the signposted Coastal Path ahead. After the last bungalow, bear left and climb towards the cliffs **C** along the edge of a field. Cross the stiles ahead but ignore a stile in the fence on your left. Use the steps to descend, then cross the footbridge in a wooded valley floor. Pass above brambles on your right.

3 Join a broad grassy track descending from an old quarry on your left, crossing a stream in the next valley bottom. Climb a wooden staircase to a stile. Follow the seaward edge of a field to reach a stile in the next corner.

4 Cross the stile and turn left, inland, as signposted. Follow the fence and hedge on your left to come to a stile in a

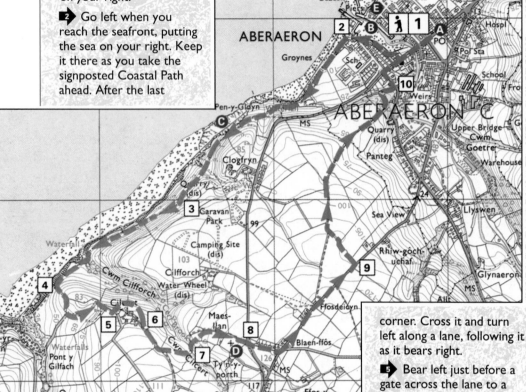

corner. Cross it and turn left along a lane, following it as it bears right.

5 Bear left just before a gate across the lane to a waymarked stile. Continue over it and beside a fence on your right to a stile in the next corner. Cross this and bear right to a stile in the far top corner, passing close to some farm buildings on your right.

6 Take the hedged path ahead until you see a waymarked stile on your left. Veer left across this and over a field to a waymark post on the edge of woodland. Go ahead over a footbridge across the shaded stream.

7 Turn left to climb a path through the trees to a stile. Continue diagonally right across a small field to a waymark post. Go right, following the hedge on your left to reach a waymarked gate in the corner, then ahead to pass a farmhouse and a church **D** on your right.

8 Cross the A487 with care. Take the lane ahead and turn left at the next road junction. Go past the road sign for Aberaeron.

9 Just before a bungalow named 'Penrhiw', turn left over a stile to follow the signposted path beside the hedge on your right. This leads to a hedged track which bends right, down into Aberaeron.

10 Go left when you reach Panteg Road. When you reach the A487, turn right and follow it back to the start (or divert left down Market Street to visit the Sea Aquarium **E**).

it could provide a link between the Pembrokeshire Coast Path to the south and the Dyfi Valley Way to the north, leading to the projected Cambrian Coast Way.

ANCIENT CHURCH

The path twice drops down into delightful, verdant, glaciated river valleys. Soon after the second of these, you strike out inland, passing the Parish Church of Henfynyw **D**, which is dedicated to St David and was, according to some experts, the site of a 6th-century church.

The route then follows a road and clear path to take you back down into Aberaeron. If you have time, you may like to divert down Market Street, then left along Cadwgan Place and right along Quay Parade to the fascinating Sea Aquarium **E**.

▶ *The well-maintained coastal path, running south from Aberaeron, offers fine views over Cardigan Bay.*

A SMUGGLERS' COVE

Prehistoric sites and the haunt of smugglers on the Ceredigion coast

▲*The climb to the cliff top is rewarded by an invigorating view before you reach the settlement at Castell Bâch. Inland, gorse (right) flowers all year but is at its best from March to June.*

This walk explores some fine coastal scenery that lies just to the south-west of the resort of New Quay. It begins from a car park at Cwmtydu **Ⓐ**, a cove at the mouth of the Afon Ffynnon-Ddewi. On occasions, storms throw up pebbles from the shingle beach to form a natural dam across the mouth of the river. Once the storm has passed, children delight in paddling in the large freshwater pool that the river forms. Both children and adults enjoy exploring the rugged sides of the cove, which are riddled with caves and exposed rock formations.

CONTRABAND

In the 18th century this spot had a more sinister reputation. Smugglers used the cove to land French brandy, which was brought in via Ireland. Despite all the best efforts of the

FACT FILE

⚹ Cwmtydu, 14 miles (22.4km) north-east of Cardigan

🗺 Pathfinder 988 (SN 25/35), grid reference SN 356575

```
miles 0   1   2   3   4   5   6   7   8   9   10 miles
kms   0 1 2 3 4 5 6 7 8 9 10 11 12 13 14 15 kms
```

◔ 1½ hours

▬ Moderately strenuous cliff climb; grassy slopes, lanes, fields and woodland paths. May be muddy in places and exposed on windy days. Walking shoes recommended

Ⓟ Car park at the start

🍴 Café and shop at Cwmtydu, open in the holiday season

🚻 Toilets at Cwmtydu

excise men, the smugglers' leader, known as Sion Cwilt because of the patchwork coat he always wore, was never captured.

A stiff climb up the side of the cove leads to cliff tops from where porpoises and seals can sometimes be seen, sporting in the waters below. Inland, there are stands of yellow gorse, which attract a variety of butterflies in summer, including painted ladies, small tortoiseshells and common skippers.

USEFUL VANTAGE POINT

Further along the route, on your left, is the site of the ancient settlement of Castell Bâch **Ⓑ**. This Iron Age earthwork occupies a high vantage point and commands sweeping

THE WALK

CWMTYDU-CASTELL BÂCH

The walk begins at the beach car park at Cwmtydu Ⓐ, 4 miles (6.4km) south-west of New Quay along the A486 then minor roads.

▶1 Facing the sea, turn right out of the car park. In the corner of the cove there is a signpost. Cross the stile in the fence just below it and take a path that zigzags up the cliff. Where this meets another path, turn left along it, keeping the sea on your left-hand side, to reach a stile in a fence.

▶2 Cross the stile and go straight on, passing Castell Bâch Ⓑ on your left. Cross a small footbridge and pass through a gap in a wall to reach another signpost.

▶3 Turn right past the farmhouse at Pen-y-graig.

Turn left through a gate and follow a farm track for 140 yards (125m) to reach a stile and gate on your left. Go left here and follow a farm track for 55 yards (50m), then turn left at a waymark and descend with a hedge, then woodland, on your left, to come to a gate.

▶4 Follow the path through the gate into the woodland. Pass a footbridge on your left and continue ahead up wooden steps signposted 'Church'. Climb through woodland with a stream below you on the left.

▶5 Cross a stile to enter the Church of St Tysilio (Eglwys Llandysiliogogo) Ⓒ. Bear right then left around the church and leave by the main gate. Turn right, then almost immediately left to reach a stile.

▶6 Cross the stile and walk along the field edge with a hedge on your right. Cross another stile and follow a farm track, with the hedge on your left-hand side, to reach a lane. Go right. At the next fork, go left down the hill.

▶7 When you reach the valley floor, turn sharp right and follow the road, past the old limekiln Ⓓ, back to the car park.

---

views that would have given plenty of warning of the approach of any aggressor. The earthen banks, once topped by timber fences, enclosed an inner circle of thatched round huts and storage places, while cattle were kept in an outer compound. The settlement, on this exposed but lovely site, was occupied between 300BC and AD100, and it is thought that as many as 40 people lived here at any one time.

Beyond Castell Bâch, the path descends into a wooded valley

▶ *In this limekiln, sturdily built of local stone, a furnace once roared away, turning calcium carbonate into lime.*

and climbs again to the remote Church of St Tysilio (Eglwys Llandysiliogogo) Ⓒ which is set within an ancient stone circle.

SAINTLY SPOT

There have been two saints by the name of Tysilio. One is thought to have been the son of Brochwel, the Prince of Powys. He was born at Pengwern — the Shrewsbury of today, which was then part of Wales — in around AD575 and, on becoming a monk, moved to a monastery in Brittany. The other Tysilio was probably the son of Corun, descended from Ceredig and Cunedda Wledig before him. One of the two — though it is not known which — came to this spot, already a sacred site, to preach Christianity.

Renovation work carried out in

◀ *The single-storey Church of St Tysilio, flanked by lines of old gravestones, stands in the lee of a small wood.*

1890 led to the discovery that the pulpit had been sited on a stone so massive that the builders of the church were unable to remove it and were forced to incorporate it into the fabric of the building.

From here, your route leads back through narrow lanes and along the valley road, following the stream back to the beach car park. Shortly before the beach, you pass an old limekiln Ⓓ. This is a reminder of a more legitimate form of coastal trading that took place here in the 18th century, alongside the smuggling.

A nature walk along the wooded slope of a glaciated valley

The last Ice Age changed the shape of many upland valleys. Mountain streams rush swiftly downhill, cutting V-shaped winding valleys as they take the line of least resistance. The crushing weight of glaciers, however, moving slowly but inexorably to the sea, shears off spurs of land, and gouges out U-shaped trenches. When the ice retreated, it left behind valleys with steep sides and flat bottoms. The Gwaun Valley is a typical example.

BROADLEAVED WOODS

The Afon Gwaun, which reaches the sea at Fishguard (Abergwaun in Welsh) 5 miles (8km) to the west, runs in just such a valley **A**. Today, broadleaved woods cling to the precipitous valley sides and the river — one of the few remaining places in Britain where the elusive otter can still be seen in the wild — winds through boggy meadows. These meadows make good pasture for fattening stock animals that have overwintered on the tops, as well as a fine habitat for wild flowers. This combination has led to the valley being designated a Site of Special Scientific Interest.

MASSIVE BEECHES

The walk begins in a car park at the hamlet of Pontfaen. The woods here contain at least 16 species of trees, including ash, birch, various thorns, hornbeam, holly, wych elm, chestnut and cherry. The trees are particularly tall on the lower slopes and on the valley floor, where the damp conditions suit alder and willow. There are also some massive beeches growing here, some of which are more than 200 years old.

The walk keeps to the valley bottom for the first half, then crosses

▲*At the start of the walk, the Afon Gwaun meanders gently through a flat valley, the wooded, steep slopes of which are home to a wide variety of wildlife, including dormice (inset), foxes and other mammals.*

FACT FILE	
✳	Pontfaen, 5 miles (8km) east of Fishguard
▣	Pathfinder 1033 (SN 03/13), grid reference SN 024339
	miles 0 1 2 3 4 5 6 7 8 9 10 miles kms 0 1 2 3 4 5 6 7 8 9 10 11 12 13 14 15 kms
🕐	Allow 1½ hours
◣	One fairly stiff climb. The lower path may be wet and muddy; waterproof footwear recommended
P	On the edge of woodland at the start
🍺	Dyffryn Arms, Pontfaen

THE WALK

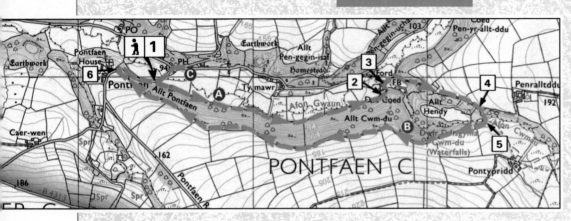

with a field on your left and the wooded valley on your right.

4 At a signpost, turn right down a narrow path. Go ahead over a rustic footbridge (slippery when wet) and up wooden steps.

5 Turn right along a waymarked path to the top of the wood. Follow this path, with the hedge on your left, past the badger setts **B**. Further on, you pass a bench at a viewpoint. The path gradually descends to come to a road.

6 Turn right to return to the car park. As an optional extension, continue on the road over the bridge and turn right to the Dyffryn Arms **C**.

GWAUN VALLEY

The walk begins at a small car park at the edge of the woodland, just to the east of Pontfaen.

1 Take the path from the back of the car park, with the wood on your right and the boundary hedge on your left. Continue along the edge of the valley floor **A** for ¾ mile (1.2km), until you reach a Pembrokeshire National Park sign for Coed Pontfaen.

2 Fork left downhill, ignoring the path climbing to your right. Go ahead past a signpost.

3 Turn right over the footbridge, and immediately step over the edge of the stream. Follow a hedged track for about 45 yards (40m) to another signpost. Turn right to climb steadily up a rough track with woodland on both sides of you. Ignore a farm access track on your right. Carry on ahead,

tributary streams and climbs to the top of the slope for the return walk. The streams descend in a series of rapids and waterfalls, and you may be able to hear them through the trees below to your right.

The woods provide food and shelter for a variety of wildlife. This is perhaps best appreciated in the spring, when wild flowers are at their best and the songs of warblers, thrushes and finches fill the air, though there is plenty to see at other

▲ *Gnarled, moss-covered trees, many of great age, flourish in the damp valley floor, while badgers dig their setts (left) near the top of the woodland path.*

times of the year. Buzzards and ravens fly overhead, and woodcocks mate and nest in the damp, open areas near the bottom of the slopes.

Mammals ranging from the dormouse to the fox make their home in the woods, but you will have to tiptoe up here at night if you wish to see the badgers who have dug the setts **B** near the perimeter hedge on the top path. However, it is perhaps best to leave these long-threatened animals alone altogether.

Fungi abound in the autumn, on the top path as well as on the wetter lower slopes. As you walk along the top path, notice how the beeches, which thrive on shallow soils, still grow to a great height, but the oaks and rowans, which do not, are somewhat poor and stunted.

A FINE VIEW

The path gradually goes downhill to the car park where you started, but it is worth making a short diversion over the bridge to the Dyffryn Arms **C**, from where you can get an excellent view of the woods across the valley floor, and then imbibe some well-earned refreshment.

▲From the summit of Bannau Sir Gaer, the awesome isolation of the lake Lyn y Fan Fach can be fully appreciated; in summer, however, the buttercup-like water-crowfoot (left) covers its surface.

Rare birds and spectacular Brecon Beacons scenery

This hill walk takes you to a remote and fascinating area surrounding the Black Mountain in the old county of Carmarthenshire, where cliffs rise to over 2,000 feet (600m) and tower dramatically above two lakes. On a clear day, there are views north of a patchwork of hill farms and native scrub oaks, and south over moorland to dark conifer plantations.

This is a truly wild area. Some of Britain's rarest birds of prey, such as red kites, peregrines and merlins, can be seen here, while buzzards and ravens are relatively common.

FACT FILE

⁎ Llanddeusant, 10 miles (16km) south of Llandovery

▱▱ Outdoor Leisure Map 12, grid reference SN 797238

miles 0 1 2 3 4 5 6 7 8 9 10 miles
kms 0 1 2 3 4 5 6 7 8 9 10 11 12 13 14 15 kms

◔ Allow 4 hours

◣ Strenuous hill walking in open country, with some steep ascents and descents. Suitable for fit and energetic walkers only; there are dangerous cliffs where children and dogs should be supervised. Use of compass advisable. Should not be attempted in poor weather. Wear rain- or chill-proof clothes and walking boots

🅿 Car park at the start, near the water board's filtration station

▥ Pub at Llanddeusant

This is largely because they are undisturbed by man, and walkers should take care to keep noise to a minimum and, for their own safety, as well as that of the nesting birds, keep away from the cliff edges. The best way to see any of these raptors is in flight. The 90-mph (124-kmh) dive of the peregrine falcon, with its black bandit-mask and barred chest, is an unforgettable sight.

The real star here, though, is the red kite. Lighter and more aerobatic than the buzzard, the kite's deeply forked tail, flashing colour and style of hunting — a flapping hover followed by a dart-like fall onto its prey — make it unmistakable. Mid-Wales is the last retreat of the native red kite in Britain, though there are more on the Continent and birds are being reintroduced from Sweden to English and Scottish sites.

LEGENDARY LAKE

The walk begins at the end of the road from Llanddeusant, and leads up a track to the legendary lake of Llyn y Fan Fach ⒶA, where long strands of flowering water-crowfoot decorate the surface in summer.

The story goes that a local farmer fell in love with a beautiful fairy who lived in the clear waters. She bore him three sons to whom she passed on some herbal remedies. They founded a long line of local healers called the Physicians of Myddfai (a nearby village). These recipes, written in the 9th-century *Red Book of Hergest*, include an infusion of foxgloves to ease angina.

Once you have climbed the long escarpment behind the lake to the ridge ⒷB, you can get a better impression of the clarity and great depth of the lake, although it is not 'bottomless', as another local legend has it! The Llanelli Water Board has used the lake as a reservoir since 1922.

On your left, a cairn marks the 2,457-foot (749-m) peak of Bannau Sir Gaer ⒸC, and to the right is the valley of the Twrch ⒹD. This long, deep 'cwm' is said to have been made by a giant boar run to earth there by King Arthur.

You descend from the peak and

THE WALK

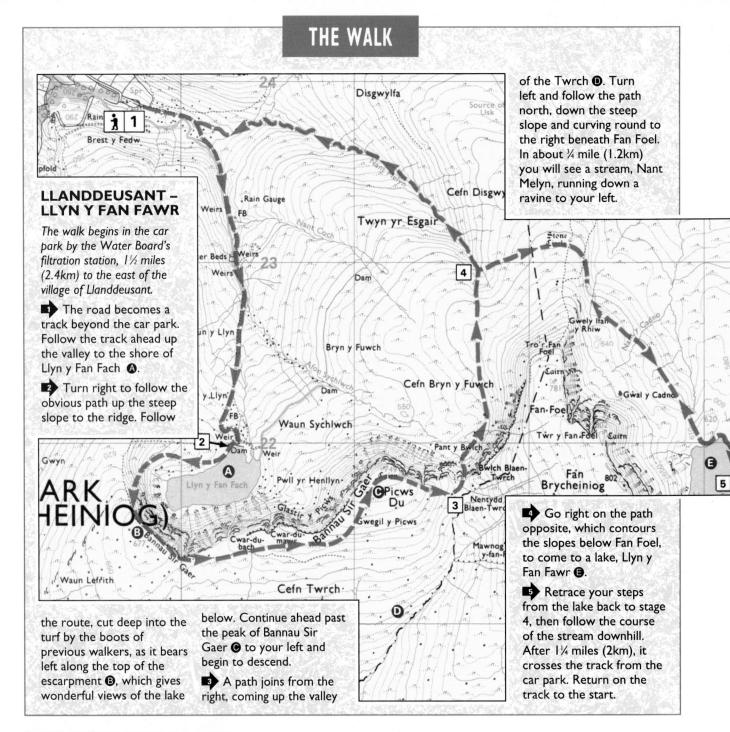

LLANDDEUSANT – LLYN Y FAN FAWR

The walk begins in the car park by the Water Board's filtration station, 1½ miles (2.4km) to the east of the village of Llanddeusant.

1 The road becomes a track beyond the car park. Follow the track ahead up the valley to the shore of Llyn y Fan Fach **A**.

2 Turn right to follow the obvious path up the steep slope to the ridge. Follow

the route, cut deep into the turf by the boots of previous walkers, as it bears left along the top of the escarpment **B**, which gives wonderful views of the lake

below. Continue ahead past the peak of Bannau Sir Gaer **C** to your left and begin to descend.

3 A path joins from the right, coming up the valley

of the Twrch **D**. Turn left and follow the path north, down the steep slope and curving round to the right beneath Fan Foel. In about ¾ mile (1.2km) you will see a stream, Nant Melyn, running down a ravine to your left.

4 Go right on the path opposite, which contours the slopes below Fan Foel, to come to a lake, Llyn y Fan Fawr **E**.

5 Retrace your steps from the lake back to stage 4, then follow the course of the stream downhill. After 1¼ miles (2km), it crosses the track from the car park. Return on the track to the start.

turn left, going round the base of Fan Foel to Llyn y Fan Fawr **E**. This lake is shallower than its sister to the west, and is in an even more secluded spot under the 2,631-foot (802-m) summit of Fan Brycheiniog.

Both lakes are home to many eels, which breed in the Sargasso Sea. After migrating across the Atlantic and up the river, they come to rest here, 1,800 feet (600m) above sea level. In drought years, they have

◄Llyn y Fan Fawr is shallower and even more isolated than its sister lake.

been seen struggling up the dry beds of ravines leading to the lake.

The last breeding pair of golden eagles in this region was killed here in the last century by an egg collector. He had them both stuffed, and the male now perches in a glass case in Swansea Museum, an institution so quaint that Dylan Thomas was moved to declare that it should be a museum exhibit in its own right.

From this spot, you follow the rock-strewn valley of a mountain stream, Nant Melyn, to the outward track not far from the start.

DYFED

A quiet and ancient corner of the Pembrokeshire coast

This walk is at its best in summer, when the cliff-tops and hedgerows bustle with wild flowers, but it has other features that will appeal all year round. There are cliffs that fascinate geologists, an old port and an island to which you can cross, as well as seabirds, seals and an ancient burial chamber.

COLOURFUL HOUSES

You begin in the village of Trevine. Many of the houses here have cement-washed roofs and coloured walls. In the main square **Ⓐ**, which is a solid slab of bare rock, stands a working long-handled pump.

A well-signposted path leads to the Pembrokeshire Coast Path and three deep bays framed by cliffs of 500-million-year-old Ordovician rock. These are folded and faulted into fascinating shapes, and wave action has eroded arches, platforms and pinnacles, visible from the winding cliff path. Fulmars nest on the high rock ledges and seals sometimes swim in the clear waters.

Beyond the bays is the bleak headland of Castell-coch **Ⓑ**, which means 'red castle'. The banks and ditches that protect the neck of this high peninsula are best seen before brambles and gorse claim the site in summer. The earthworks date from around 300BC, and were made by tribes fleeing Roman rule in Gaul.

This type of fort suited new arrivals; there are two more Castell-cochs along the coast within 5 miles (8km) of this one. The settlers soon moved inland, or joined forces to hold larger sites like Garn Fawr,

FACT FILE

- ✳ Trevine, 7½ miles (12km) south-west of Fishguard, off the A487

- Pathfinder 1032 (SM 83/93), grid reference SM 840325

  miles 0 1 2 3 4 5 6 7 8 9 10 miles
  kms 0 1 2 3 4 5 6 7 8 9 10 11 12 13 14 15 kms

- ◷ Allow 3 to 4 hours

- Clifftop and field paths. Some steep slopes. Rocky in places. Walking boots recommended

- 🅿 In streets near the start

- 🆃 Infrequent bus services from Fishguard, St David's and Haverfordwest to Trevine. The South Wales Tourism Council has details, Tel. (01267) 7557

- 🏚 Pub in Trevine

▲*A view across Abercastle Bay to Ynys y Castell and the castle after which the village is most probably named. Rock samphire (inset) is impervious to salt spray and grows here on the cliffs.*

which was occupied for up to 1,000 years and dominates the north-eastern horizon throughout the walk.

The route follows the rocky headland around to the old port of Abercastle **Ⓒ**. This natural harbour was once known as 'Bay of Boats', from the days when sloops plied the coastal trade. Locals exported wool, slate, beeswax and preserved fish, and imported essentials such as coal and limestone. A set of derelict limekilns still lines the quayside. On the other side of the cove, the path climbs past former fishermen's cottages, one of which has several specimens of a rare, wild tree mallow growing in its sheltered garden.

ANCIENT CROMLECH

If the tide permits, it is worth crossing the rocky causeway to Ynys y Castell **Ⓓ**, and scrambling to the top. In season, the slopes are carpeted with wild flowers, and to the south-west there is a fine view of Careg Sampson (Sampson's Stone) **Ⓔ**, which resembles a giant tortoise crawling up the hill. This cromlech was built about 5,000 years ago, by people of a New Stone Age culture

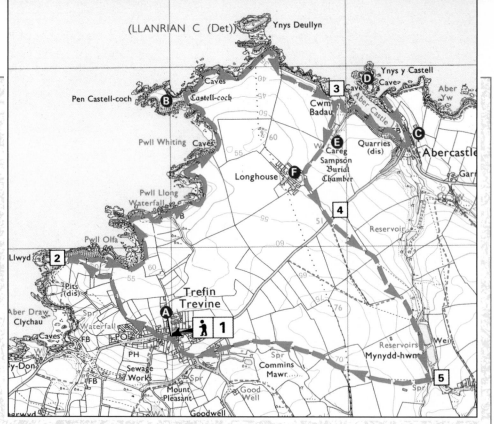

THE WALK

TREVINE – ABERCASTLE

The walk begins in the main square **A** *of Trevine.*

1 Walk away from the church, down the main street, and turn right down a signposted footpath, which winds down to reach the Pembrokeshire Coast Path.

2 Turn right and follow the path along the coast for about 2½ miles (4km) past Castell-coch **B** and eventually down to a road. Turn left to cross the stream, then left again up the coastal path to explore Abercastle **C** and Ynys y Castell **D**. Retrace your steps back to the road and along the coastal path, which winds through a valley.

3 On the other side of the valley, turn left on the field-edge path to Careg

Sampson **E**. Continue ahead to Longhouse Farm **F**, and turn left along the farm track to a road.

4 Cross and take the path that bears half-left across the field opposite to its far left corner. Bear

slightly right on this path and continue to the reservoirs. Walk along the field edge, with the reservoirs on your left.

5 Where the wall bends right, turn right uphill, and through another two fields

on a clear path. Continue on a farm track to a road, and go straight on. When the road bends left, continue ahead on a footpath to another road. Turn right to return to your starting point.

◄Careg Sampson, with its 3-ton capstone, is an impressive structure that was once part of a burial chamber. In spring and summer (below) the clifftops can be covered with delightful carpets of flowers.

that once covered western Europe. It was originally covered with smaller stones, earth and turf, but this shell has been eroded away. Now, only its bare bones remain; massive, sculptural and mysterious.

Legend attributes it to a local boy made good. St Sampson was a Celtic Christian who died around AD600. When most of Britain was still pagan, he was Abbot of Caldey Island, near Tenby, and of a monastery in Brittany. A great missionary, his fame spread as far as Switzerland and Italy, where some

of his bones remain as holy relics.

Sampson supposedly placed the 3-ton capstone in position using only faith and his little finger. This prodigious digit is said to lie buried on the island opposite. The story dates from the 10th century, when the Celtic and Catholic churches merged, and the Celts needed to claim miracles on behalf of their saints to maintain their status.

Beyond the stone circle is Longhouse Farm **F**, whose core structure was once a longhouse, where family and livestock shared the shelter of a single roof. This form of habitation is a legacy from the centuries when Pembrokeshire was colonized by Norsemen.

ANCIENT WAYS

The hedgerows bordering the paths on your return to Trevine are equally ancient. Stones from the fields have been added to their broad banks. Archaeologists claim that some are part of the original Celtic field systems, which were hundreds of years old by the time of Christ.

and the Bristol Channel. Long fault lines cut the rocky coast into dangerous but fascinating crevasses, some up to 100 feet (30m) deep.

SANDY BEACH

Heather, gorse and bracken grow in abundance, along with sea pinks, kale, ox-eye daisies and, very unusual in this type of habitat, snake's-head fritillaries. Cormorants, shags and gulls sail past you at eye-level. Eventually, you arrive at a cliff overlooking an enticing sandy bay ❻. The scramble down is worth it for those who like to swim. The bay here is calmer than at Manorbier, and there is no danger of being hit by a surfboard.

The route heads inland from here. Before following it, take some time to admire the striking cliffs of Old

to do was 'write, write, write', and how she sat on the sands screwing up her courage to tell her parents of the career she had chosen.

SURFERS' PARADISE

Today, the beach ❸ provides inspiration for surfers, who come from miles around. Undersea rock formations force up a steady supply of large waves. The route leaves the castle and beach behind for the Pembrokeshire Coast Path, which leads to the quaintly-named headland, the Priest's Nose ❹. The outline of the rocks is said to resemble the imposing profile of the Archdeacon de Barri, but as no picture of Gerald exists, the story

▲*Although its domed roof is somewhat overgrown, the cylindrical dovecote is otherwise in fine condition.*

is probably fanciful.

A gentle slope leads up to the half-covered remains of King's Quoit ❺, a Neolithic burial chamber that dates from around 3000BC and was fashioned from the local, fossil-encrusted, red sandstone. Its huge capstone rivals any other in Wales for size, but since this cromlech is partially covered by earth — as they all were originally — it cannot compete as the most spectacular.

The coast path comes into its own beyond the cromlech, with views far and wide across Carmarthen Bay

▲*After leaving Manorbier, the route takes you to King's Quoit, a Neolithic burial chamber with a huge capstone. It is perched above the pounding surf of Manorbier Bay (below).*

Castle Head **G** above the beach to the east. There is a Celtic hillfort dating from 300BC on the headland. Its builders skilfully included the abrupt changes in ground level as well as geological faults when they fortified the site. The headland has formed part of a Royal Artillery range for many years and access is

▶ *From Priest's Nose headland you follow the Pembrokeshire Coast Path eastwards to a remote bay at Presipe (right). In places the rocky coast has vertical fault lines (left) and there are views beyond to Old Castle Head.*

very strictly controlled.

The return to Manorbier is along a well-signposted footpath and quiet country lanes through open country, then along a minor road. There are memorable views of the church, castle and village for a good part of the way after you pass Hill Farm.

Back in the village, a short climb leads to St James **H**, the Norman church on a hill across from the castle. The church is entered down steps through a vaulted porch, in which there are the remains of a medieval painting. Inside, there are stone effigies of various lords of the manor, one of whom died on a crusade to the Holy Land.

The Bishop's Palace at St David's, now in ruins, was denied to Gerald.

Sylvestor the Wildman

Gerald de Barri, Manorbier's most famous son, had many names and titles, as befitted a man of so many accomplishments and interests. During his 77 years (1146-1223) he was a priest, scholar, lecturer on law at the Universities of Paris and Bologna, advisor on Welsh politics to three English kings, a royal chaplain, and a tutor to the young princes who later ruled as Kings Richard I and John. He was also the author of 17 books, some of them still in print today.

His father was a Norman knight and his mother the issue of a political marriage between a powerful Norman invader and a Welsh princess. His uncle was Bishop of St David's, and Gerald declared early in life that he wished to follow in his relative's footsteps.

His ambition did not stop there. Gerald firmly believed Wales should have its own archbishop, and saw himself as the ideal candidate. Recognizing this could split his kingdom, Henry II denied Gerald the bishopric of St David's, though he had been unanimously elected to the post by the canons.

This occurred five years after the murder of Thomas à Becket in Canterbury Cathedral, and Gerald was advised to accept the decision. He found this impossible to do and, to keep an eye on him, Henry summoned Gerald to court and kept him there.

He warned his sons not to let 'Sylvestor the Wildman', as he contemptuously nicknamed Gerald, gain power in Wales, and both Richard and John, though they offered him other bishoprics in England, denied him St David's.

Eventually, Gerald took his case to the Pope. At first, he was heard with sympathy in Rome, but emissaries from the king and Canterbury bribed the pontiff to deny him support.

On his return, an edict was issued against him, declaring any further attempt to pursue his claim an act of rebellion. Gerald spent his last years in hiding. No-one knows where he died, or whether he really was, as legend has it, buried at St David's.

DYFED

Explore the limestone landscape around a great natural fortress

Perched on sheer limestone cliffs, the brooding ruins of Carreg Cennen Castle cast a foreboding shadow over the peaceful Cennen Valley. It is a site redolent of history in a landscape of wild grandeur.

This walk begins by heading across the land south of the massive rock of Carreg Cennen Ⓐ, whose impressive bulk dominates the skyline throughout. Three of its sides are 300-foot (91-m) precipices, natural defences that have historically made the site attractive to settlers.

PLANTS AND BIRDS

You walk down into a valley by hedgerows with a colourful profusion of lords and ladies, dog violets, stitchwort, wood sorrel, celandine and yellow rattle. The area is a nature reserve and is rich in bird life. Pied flycatchers, redstarts, wood warblers, woodpeckers, treecreepers and handsome nuthatches are all found here.

FACT FILE

※ Carreg Cennen, 4 miles (6.4km) south-east of Llandeilo

▦ Pathfinder 1083 (SN 61/71) or Outdoor Leisure Map 12, grid reference SN 666193

miles 0 1 2 3 4 5 6 7 8 9 10 miles
kms 0 1 2 3 4 5 6 7 8 9 10 11 12 13 14 15 kms.

◷ Allow 2½ hours

▬ Mostly tarmac lanes, farm tracks and footpaths. Some paths can be muddy and are steep, so good walking boots are recommended

🅿 Castle car park at the start

🍴 Restaurant, tea-room and shop at Carreg Cennen Castle

🚾 In the car park at the start

🏰 Carreg Cennen Castle is always open. Those wishing to explore the cave beneath the castle should hire a torch and buy a guide book from the shop at Carreg Cennen Farm (open daily, 8.30am-8pm) before starting the walk

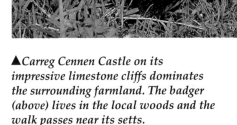

▲*Carreg Cennen Castle on its impressive limestone cliffs dominates the surrounding farmland. The badger (above) lives in the local woods and the walk passes near its setts.*

The track follows a stream past the source of the Llwchwr, or Loughor. The river Ⓑ issues rather unromantically from a water board regulation point, though, in May, the banks on either side are carpeted with spotted orchids. Around 17 miles (27km) of underground passageways lead from the cave.

Nearby are the remains of 19th-century limekilns Ⓒ, where rock was processed to reduce the acidity of the peaty soils on the surrounding uplands. In the deep, tree-lined ravines along the path are the entrances to badger setts, piled high with soil and old bedding.

THE WALK

CARREG CENNEN – LLYGAD LLWCHWR

The walk begins from the castle's car park, near a farm at the end of the lane from Trapp to Carreg Cennen Castle.

1 Head away from Carreg Cennen **A** and turn left along the lane. Turn first left into a narrow lane and go downhill, following the lane as it bears left.

2 Just before Pantyffynnont cottage, turn right over a waymarked step stile. Go straight on down field paths to a step stile, and fork left to another stile. Bear left to head for the footbridge over a stream.

3 Continue uphill across the field to a stile in the top corner, heading to the right-hand side of the buildings on the skyline.

4 At the buildings, turn right onto a farm track. Continue across a stream and over a cattle grid. After the track bends left uphill, turn left over a waymarked step stile and follow a farm track to the next step stile. Cross onto some stepping stones, then bear right at a fork to follow the stream.

5 Cross a step stile and bear right uphill on the main track past the source of the River Loughor **B** on your right and some limekilns **C** on the left. Continue on the track, then follow a path across the field to a step stile on the far side. Turn right to cross the field to a step stile into a lane.

6 Turn left along the lane. Where the lane bends right, fork left and proceed straight on past Beddau'r Derwyddon **D** over to the right. Continue on the clear path for ¾ mile (1.2km), crossing step stiles, to a fork. Bear left to the bottom of the hill, then turn sharp left. Turn right onto a stone track. Continue for about 300 yards (270m), until you reach a footbridge.

7 Cross the bridge. Turn right, then sharp left uphill towards Carreg Cennen Castle **E**. When the path joins a narrow tarmac path below the castle, turn left to visit the ruins. Retrace your steps to the path junction. Turn left and follow the path through a kissing-gate back to the farm and the car park, where the walk began.

Well-worn badger 'highways' cross the shady woodland floor.

The path runs along the lower slopes of the Black Mountain, about 1,000 feet (300m) above sea level, with views back across the valley. At Beddau'r Derwyddon **D** are long, low, grassed-over mounds known as Druid's Graves. They are medieval pillow mounds, man-made warrens constructed where the soil was too thin for rabbits to burrow.

ACROSS MOORLAND

The open woodland and moor on the return to Carreg Cennen is the haunt of short-eared owls, ravens and kestrels. Buzzards circle over the tree tops, or soar with wings outstretched, on the look out for rabbits, voles or carrion; their mewing cry is instantly recognizable. The occasional red kite may also be seen, circling high on the rising thermals over the remote uplands.

The first Carreg Cennen Castle **E** was probably built by the Welsh chieftain, Prince Rhys ap Gruffydd, near the end of the 12th century. It was taken without a fight by Edward I in 1277. Most of what is visible today dates from the English occupation, which lasted well over a century. Some chroniclers say the castle fell to Owain Glyndwr early in the 15th century; others say the garrison — its natural defences being so good that less than 20 men could defend it — held out until the rebellion ended in 1410.

The castle was a Lancastrian stronghold in the Wars of the Roses, but was surrendered in 1462. Soon afterwards, 500 men with picks and crowbars spent 110 days ruining the castle so that it could no longer be used. There is enough left, though, to give an indication of its layout and some spectacular viewpoints.

The castle has its own water supply in a cave in the rock beneath. This is reached via a 200-foot (60-m), vaulted passage, made by covering over a path down the rock face. The passage is dimly lit by narrow slits in the outer wall, but those wishing to explore should take a torch or risk bumping their heads.

Stewardship of the ruins passed back and forth between Welsh and English noble families until the 1960s, when it was accidentally included in the sale of some agricultural land. It now belongs to Castle Farm in the valley below, where the walk ends.

◄ *Having run underground, the River Loughor (Llygad Llwchwr) emerges above ground from this cave.*

four years of his life. Thomas, whose rich, dense imagery won him early acclaim, is perhaps best remembered for a prose work, the radio play *Under Milk Wood*. It is tempting to see echoes of Llareggub, the play's fictional setting, in Laugharne, though many scholars believe the work was based on Newquay, in Cardiganshire.

FAIRYTALE CASTLE

The walk begins at Laugharne Castle Ⓐ, a fairytale ruin with ivy-clad walls studded with blue periwinkles. The site was originally

---

A walk around Dylan Thomas's home in a sleepy seaside town

▲*Built as a garage for Laugharne's first car, this shed was where Dylan Thomas wrote* **Under Milk Wood**. *It overlooks the Taf Estuary, where the dab (top right) is a common flatfish.*

Laugharne (pronounced Larn) nestles snugly in the folds of the Carmarthenshire hills, overlooking the broad golden sands of the Taf Estuary. During the 16th century, it was the haunt of pirates who preyed on ships in the bustling Bristol Channel. Laugharne was a thriving medieval port; its fabulous Norman castle, built on a site occupied by the last Prince of South Wales, still dominates the ancient town.

Despite its colourful history and intrinsic beauty, Laugharne is better known today as the place where the poet Dylan Thomas spent the last

---

FACT FILE

※ Laugharne, 14 miles (22.5km) south-west of Carmarthen, on the A4066

os Pathfinders 1081 (SN 21/31) and 1105 (SN 20/30), grid reference SN 301107

miles 0 1 2 3 4 5 6 7 8 9 10 miles
kms 0 1 2 3 4 5 6 7 8 9 10 11 12 13 14 15 kms

◔ Allow about 3 hours

▭ Coastal and woodland paths, farm tracks and tarmac. No steep climbs; suitable for all ages. Some sections may be muddy after rain

P Free parking at the start near Laugharne Castle

🍺 Several pubs in Laugharne

🍴 Restaurants in Laugharne and a tea-room at the Boat House

🏰 The Boat House is open April-October, daily, 10am-5pm, and November-March, daily, 10.30am-3pm

THE WALK

LAUGHARNE CASTLE – ROCHE CASTLE – SIR JOHN'S HILL

The walk begins from the car park near Laugharne Castle **A** *in the centre of the town.*

1 Head towards the water. Cross a footbridge and follow the coastal path below the castle.

2 Fork left up a rocky path leading to some concrete steps. At the top of the steps, bear right past Dylan Thomas's writing shed **B**. Continue on the tarmac path.

3 After about 50 yards (45m), descend some steps to visit the Boat House **C**. Return to the tarmac path and turn right to follow Dylan's Walk **D** into woodland. Cross a tarmac lane and continue along the woodland path, keeping left on the main route at a fork.

4 At a step stile, cross into a field. Follow the line of the hedge to your right. Head for a step stile in the hedgerow behind a tree on the far side of the field. Cross the stile and field towards a farm. Go over a step stile and past a ruined building. Continue through the farmyard to the left of the farmhouse. Go up the farm lane, and continue through a gate.

5 Shortly after a road joins from your right, turn left, then bear right, downhill, on the road.

6 Enter the graveyard of St Martin's Church **E** through a kissing-gate at the end of the stone wall on your right. On the far side of the church are some steps. Bear left over the footbridge into the modern burial ground. Go uphill to pass Dylan Thomas's grave in the centre of the graveyard. Exit through a kissing-gate in the centre of the hedge at the top and turn right along a farm track. Continue downhill to a tarmac road.

7 Turn right. Take the next left to pass Sea View **F** on your right. Turn right into Market Lane. Continue, past the Town Hall **G** on your right, to the main road.

8 Go straight over the crossroads and downhill. Bear right, then turn left over a stone road-bridge. Continue on the road, bearing right onto a main road at The Lacques **H**. At a fork beside a cottage, bear left onto a track. Take a narrow footpath to the right of a house, over a footbridge, and continue to an open field and the site of Roche Castle **J**.

9 Turn left and follow the line of the hedge to a step stile. Cross and go between some buildings to a fork. Bear left to reach a

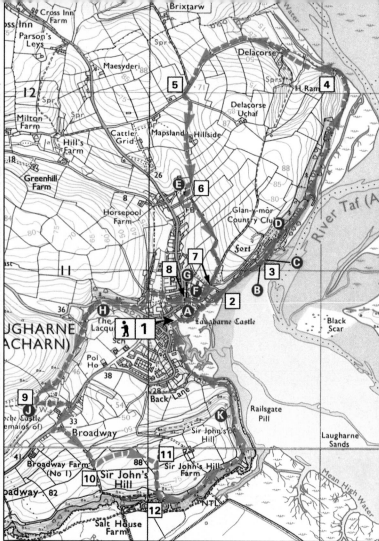

main road. Turn right for about 200 yards (180m), then go sharp left alongside a metal garage onto a waymarked footpath. Continue through the gate. At a second gate, turn right over a stile into a field and go uphill, following the line of the hedge into the next field.

10 After about 30 yards (27m), turn left into the adjacent field. Bear left to follow the line of the hedge around the field, heading for the gated opening in the stone wall opposite.

Go through, then diagonally right, heading for a waymarked opening at the top of the field.

11 Cross the stone step stile and follow the path down to the bottom right-hand corner of the field. Continue down the footpath. At a fork, bear left. Continue past a ruin to a T-junction of paths.

12 Turn left and follow the woodland path around Sir John's Hill **K** towards Laugharne. Turn left at a tarmac lane and return to the car park.

---

fortified by the Romans, and later by Rhys ap Gruffydd, who was the last Prince of South Wales.

Laugharne Castle was captured twice by the Welsh in the 13th century, and was remodelled, with Tudor embellishments, at the close of the 16th century by Sir John Perrot, High Admiral and reputed half-brother of Queen Elizabeth I. In the Civil War, the Royalist castle was destroyed by Cromwell's forces.

Just beyond the castle, looking out across the broad estuary, is an inconspicuous wooden shed **B**. This belongs to the Boat House, and was built out over the cliff-edge on stilts in the early 1900s. The shack was the garage of the first-ever motor vehicle to be seen in Laugharne. The car terrorized the local draught horses and convinced at least one inhabitant that Satan himself had come. Undeterred, she armed herself with a pitchfork and charged off in pursuit of the green Wolseley.

In the late spring of 1949, Mrs Margaret Taylor, Dylan Thomas's generous patroness, purchased the house and the poet turned the garage into his 'workshack'. A damp, draughty, overgrown place, it was hardly comfortable, but it was

◄*Laugharne Castle, once painted by Turner, has two 13th-century towers. The interior of Thomas's workshack (above) gives the impression that the writer has just slipped out to the pub.*

the path. Near the shoreline stands a more ominous ruin, known as Burnt House. According to local legend, it was deliberately destroyed after a murder was committed there.

The walk through the shady graveyard of St Martin's Church ⓔ winds beneath a canopy of venerable yews through a tangle of vegetation, crumbling gravestones and fallen angels. The beautiful church, which dates from the 14th century, is one of the earliest in the area. It was probably built by Sir Guy de Brian, Edward III's Lord High Admiral. The path crosses a bridge to a modern burial

peaceful. 'You have given me life', wrote Thomas to Mrs Taylor, 'and now I am going to live it'.

The path leads down to the Boat House ⓒ, which Thomas called 'my sea-shaken house on a breakneck of rocks', a three-storey cottage tucked into the base of red sandstone cliffs. After the poet's premature death, the house stood empty for many years until 1975, when it was opened as a memorial to him.

DYLAN'S WALK

The route continues along Dylan's Walk ⓓ. Originally known as Cliff Walk, it was renamed in 1958, the year *Under Milk Wood* was first performed in Laugharne. Across the 'dab-filled bay' to your right are the fertile, checkerboard hills of Carmarthenshire. The ivy-choked remains of cottages are scattered through the wood along the side of

◄*The Boat House, bought for Thomas by Margaret Taylor, wife of historian A J P Taylor, is now a museum to the poet. Parts of the old town, such as Market Lane (right), are little changed.*

Dylan Thomas

Augustus John's portrait of Dylan Thomas hangs in the National Museum in Cardiff.

The son of an English teacher and a farmer's daughter, Dylan Thomas was born in Swansea in 1914. From his parents, he imbibed a fascination for language — his father read him Shakespeare as bedtime stories — and a love of the Welsh countryside; his visits to his maternal grandparents' farm are fondly remembered in his poem *Fern Hill*.

He was a prolific writer in his adolescence, and published his first volume, *18 Poems*, in 1934. Most of the lyrical, Romantic poems he wrote existed, at least in embryo form, before he moved to London in 1935. He married in 1936, and for the rest of his life he struggled to support his growing family and his fondness for socializing.

In 1949, he moved to Laugharne, where he worked intensely in his 'water and tree room on the cliff' or slipped quietly away along the cliff path for a relaxing drink at Brown's Hotel. During this period he wrote *Under Milk Wood*, but composed little published poetry.

Reading tours of the United States offered him a financial lifeline — he was deeply in debt to his friends and to the Inland Revenue. He found the tours exhausting, not least because he was continually plied with whisky. Though Thomas liked to drink, he had no head for strong liquor and kept to beer when he was at home in Wales.

His fourth tour of the States, in November 1953, was intended to take him to California, and a meeting with Igor Stravinsky, with whom he hoped to create an opera. However, after a reception in New York, he fell into a coma and died. The verdict of the doctor who wrote the death certificate, that the 39-year-old poet died of an 'insult to the brain', left open the question of whether an overdose of alcohol had killed him, or whether it was a mixture of drink and medicines.

▲The Town Hall's clock tower inspired an image in Under Milk Wood.

when Myfanwy Price dreams of 'her lover, tall as the town clock-tower'.

Further on, the narrow lane ⓗ that winds along the banks of a murmuring stream has the curious name, The Lacques, which means a moist or splashy place. At one time, there were several wells here, rising from springs beneath the tree-lined banks. These springs were much frequented during the Victorian era, when the water was credited with remarkable restorative powers.

ROCHE CASTLE

Trees and overgrown hedgerows give way to open farmland and the site of Roche Castle ⓙ, which according to local stories has a subterranean tunnel connecting it with Laugharne Castle. It fell into disrepair, and masonry was taken to build new houses at Broadway; the ancient stones can be seen in buildings near the road. The local inhabitants of Laugharne used to gather among the ruins of Roche Castle, which was once owned by the Perrot family, to play bowls, dance and watch cockfights.

WILD FLOWERS

The walk continues up through sloping fields, then passes through mature woods. Wall pennywort, red campion, hart's tongue fern, cuckoo pint, wood anemone, ragged robin and delicate spotted orchid crowd the edges of the narrow path.

The return track leaves Sir John's Hill ⓚ, where Sir John Perrot planned to build a house to watch the activities of the pirates. This hill can be seen from Dylan Thomas's own window, and it inspired him to write his first poem from the work-shack, a musing on mortality that begins, '*Over Sir John's Hill*
The hawk on fire hangs still'.

▼Curving between low hills, the broad estuary of the Afon Taf is spectacular whether the tide is low, as here, or high.

ground, the final resting place of Dylan Thomas. His simple, white wooden cross contrasts sharply with the grander headstones made of carved marble that surround it.

As you return through the town, the route passes Sea View ⓕ, a simplistic doll's house of a building, its three storeys of rooms piled neatly on top of one another. Thomas lived here for some time with his wife, Caitlin, and their children.

FAMOUS CLOCK

As you cross King Street, the Town Hall and jail ⓖ is to your right. A building of considerable antiquity, it was rebuilt in 1745. Its white clock tower features in *Under Milk Wood*,

DYFED

Explore the country around the oldest university town in Wales

Lampeter is an ancient market town at the confluence of the Afon Teifi and the Afon Dulas. The rivers meander through meadows beside old railway embankments that blaze, in season, with a profusion of wild flowers. More than 400 feet (120m) above the valley floor, an Iron Age fort affords panoramic views of the rolling green hills of central Dyfed.

The walk begins in St Thomas's Square **Ⓐ**, originally an area of commonland owned by the freemen of the borough. In 1285, Edward I granted the Lord of Dryslwyn his permission to hold a fair and market in the town; by 1800, there were eight fairs a year trading horses, horned cattle, sheep and pigs.

DROVERS' INNS

The weekly market is still held here, though it is a far cry from the 18th century, when corn, butter, cheese and poultry were bought and sold, dogs and rats raked through piles of refuse and the destitute wandered between haggling traders, bearing

on their right sleeves the badge of a pauper, 'L.P.' (Lampeter Poor).

The High Street **Ⓑ**, dominated by the Victorian town hall and St Peter's Church (rebuilt in 1869), has been a bustling thoroughfare for centuries. It was a main drove road to England. Inns and ale houses sprang up along the route, and town life was coloured by 'bloody frays

---

FACT FILE

✳ Lampeter, on the A485 and the A482

▱ Pathfinders 989 (SN 45/55) and 1012 (SN 44/54), grid reference SN 576479

```
miles 0  1  2  3  4   5   6   7   8   9   10 miles
kms 0 1 2 3 4 5 6 7 8 9 10 11 12 13 14 15 kms
```

◐ Allow 2½ hours

▬ Easy walking on footpaths, woodland paths and narrow tarmac lanes

🅿 Car park at the start

🍴 Pubs, restaurants, cafés and shops in Lampeter

[WC] St Thomas's Street

Ⅰ For tourist information, Tel (01974) 298144

▲ *The quadrangle of St David's University College, founded to educate men for the Anglican ministry. Hedge woundwort (inset) flowers in shady places during July and August.*

and assaults, drunkenness and blaspheming'. Retribution was swift — six hours in the stocks cooled most tempers, and the whipping post, which stood near the town hall, was the source of endless entertainment.

St David's University College **Ⓒ** was founded in 1822 by Bishop Burgess, the Bishop of St David's, for the education of the clergy. It was granted a charter to confer Bachelor of Arts degrees in 1863.

▼ *Surrounded by farmland, Lampeter is still an important market town.*

THE WALK

LAMPETER – CASTELL ALLT-GOCH

Begin at the car park in St Thomas's Square **A**.

1 From the north end of the car park, farthest from the church, walk along St Thomas's Street. At a T-junction, turn right along the High Street **B**. Turn left into College Street. After about 50 paces, turn right into the grounds of St David's College **C**. After visiting the motte and bailey **D**, return to College Street and continue to the right. Turn right into the lane running along the far side of the rugby ground. Follow this lane down, over a cattle grid and onto a farm track, then uphill to the farm.

2 Turn left onto the footpath immediately in front of the first farm building. Continue with a line of trees to your right. At the corner, bear right through a gate onto the main path through Mount Pleasant Wood **E**. Continue uphill to a crossing track. Go straight ahead over a stile and across fields, skirting the edge of the woodland on your left, to a pair of gates.

3 Go through the left entrance, and continue uphill. Turn left over the next step-stile to walk around the base of Castell Allt-goch **F**. Return to the path, cross it and head straight on towards the wire fence at the bottom of the field. Go through a gap in the fence, then over the right-hand one of two gates. Head downhill towards a farm. Keep the farm to your left, and continue on to turn right along the farm track. Go through a gate and follow the track down to a lane above the River Teifi **G**.

4 Turn right and continue along the lane for approximately 1½ miles (2.4km). Turn right at the end. Turn left into New Street and follow it back to the car park.

The earliest buildings on the site are the neo-Gothic chapel and the students' accommodation, set around a quadrangle with a fountain. The secluded beauty of the college's setting, on the banks of the Afon Dulas, provides an intimate and peaceful academic atmosphere.

The mound to the east of the

◀*Although partially covered by gorse, the earthworks of Castell Allt-goch, an old hill fort, are still clearly visible.*

quadrangle is a Norman motte and bailey **D**, thought to have been built by King Stephen. It was destroyed in 1137 and subsequently rebuilt. In 1403 it survived the guerilla warfare of Owain Glyndwr.

RIVERSIDE LANE

Leaving Lampeter behind, the route leads up through Mount Pleasant Wood **E**, mixed woodland of beech, oak, larch and Douglas firs. Among the birds found here are coal tits, willow tits, marsh tits, long-tailed tits, bullfinches, greenfinches and redstarts, which are instantly recognizable by their fiery red tails.

Castell Allt-goch **F**, at just over 800 feet (240m) above sea level, is an impressively sited hill fort defended by two encircling banks and ditches. Within these ramparts, circular huts with thatched roofs and walls of basketwork wattle or rough stone, would have provided shelter for a people who spoke the Brythonic language, a forerunner of Welsh. The way downhill follows the route along which their farm carts once trundled over deeply rutted tracks.

The lane from Llanfair Clydogau, which returns you to the town, runs parallel with the Afon Teifi **G**, a famous trout and salmon river which rises in the mountains to the north-east. Light beech hedges entwined with honeysuckle and wild roses line the lane, and on the banks grow foxgloves, campions, violets, woundwort and stitchwort.

Visit a ruined abbey and two lakes set in tranquil pastureland

The towering ruins of Talley Abbey dramatically punctuate one of Wales's most peaceful landscapes. The stark tower arches, standing on the watershed of the Rivers Towy and Cothi, dominate two magnificent lakes set among rolling green hills and woodland.

The walk begins in Talley, heading off first into the countryside, and taking in the ruins at the end. Beyond the 18th-century Talley House, quiet country lanes lead up from the valley floor, between

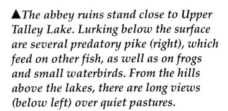

▲*The abbey ruins stand close to Upper Talley Lake. Lurking below the surface are several predatory pike (right), which feed on other fish, as well as on frogs and small waterbirds. From the hills above the lakes, there are long views (below left) over quiet pastures.*

FACT FILE

✳ Talley (Talyllychau), 6 miles (9.6km) north of Llandeilo, on the B4302

🗺 Pathfinder 1036 (SN 63/73), grid reference SN 635327

miles 0 1 2 3 4 5 6 7 8 9 10 miles
kms 0 1 2 3 4 5 6 7 8 9 10 11 12 13 14 15 kms

🕐 Allow 2½ hours

▬ Some fairly steep ascents and descents on mixture of lanes and fields, moor and forestry tracks. Good walking shoes or boots recommended

🅿 Outside Talley Abbey or Edwinsford Arms

🍴 Edwinsford Arms, Talley

WC Near the abbey

ℹ Tourist information in Llandovery, Tel. (01550) 20693

ancient hedgerows of beech, oak and holly and overhanging evergreen clumps of hart's tongue fern.

You climb through shadowy woodland, which attracts many butterflies, including the comma, speckled wood and delightful silver-washed fritillary. The path emerges onto high, open farmland which throbs with insect life in summer, prey for countless spiders and the handsome golden-ringed dragonfly, which patrols its territory along the woodland edge. Coarse mountain grasses are dotted with mountain pansies and harebells. Below is a vista of emerald fields.

EDWINSFORD

A long, broad avenue of oaks that stretches away to the north was once the drive to Edwinsford, which stands above a bend of the Afon Cothi. Edwinsford was the ancestral home of the Williams family, prominent figures in Carmarthenshire politics in the 18th and 19th centuries. Built partly in the style of an elegant French chateau, it was

TALLEY ABBEY

The walk begins from the car park of the Edwinsford Arms in Talley.

1 Turn left downhill to the T-junction. Turn right. At the right bend, turn left into a narrow lane and continue to a fork just before the white cottages.

2 Fork right onto a steep concrete track. Turn back sharp right at the next turn-off. Continue onto a forest track. About 10 paces after it bends sharp right, turn left onto a narrow woodland path. Cross a step-stile and follow the path out of the trees and across open fields, keeping the woodland on your left.

3 Cross a stile and small stream then cut diagonally right across the field, heading for the far corner. Cross a step-stile and cut diagonally right again to a stile in the corner. Go straight ahead, the hedge to your right, across the fields, passing the ruin on the right. Follow the path ahead with a woodland fence to your right, to a step-stile at the edge of the forestry. Cross a stile and bear left, then right along the field-edge. Go through two fields, and bear right along the headland of the second field to the corner, then bear left through the gap downhill, heading for the gate out into the lane.

4 Turn left. At the T-junction, turn right. Continue to the main road. Turn right, past Talley Lakes **Ⓐ**. Immediately after the Talley nameplate, turn right onto a footpath to a revolving gate.

5 Go through and follow the path into the graveyard of St Michael's Church **Ⓑ**. Continue past the church to the lane and turn left to the abbey **Ⓒ**. From the abbey, turn left and follow the lane back to the start.

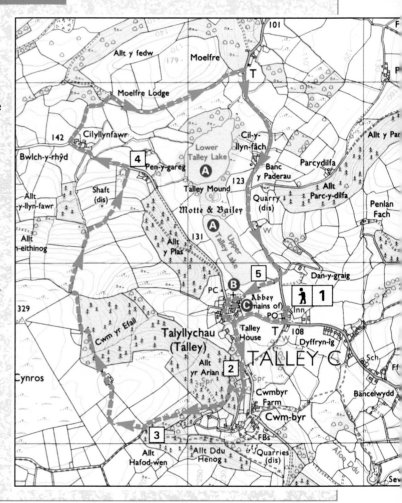

occupied during World War II by Polish refugees, who grew mushrooms under the floorboards. Today, the old house lies abandoned.

A road leads above Talley's twin lakes **Ⓐ**, rich mineral pools formed in glacial hollows. One drains to the north, the other to the south. Between them, hidden by trees, is a motte, whose origins are obscure.

The lower lake is a nature reserve. Archaeological studies of pollen deposits in the mud have given scientists an accurate picture of the change in vegetation at the dawning of the Bronze Age, when oak, ash, hazel and elm were felled to provide farmland.

The lakes offer an ideal habitat for cormorant, great crested grebe, tufted duck, coot and mute swan. Their crystal clear waters are brightened by floating water-lilies, beneath which lurk massive pike.

You re-enter Talley close to St Michael's Church **Ⓑ**, which dates from 1772. A classic bell-cote church with flagged floors, its simple, timeless beauty was augmented in the 1980s by a stained glass window, donated by a local quarry owner.

Just to the south are the remains of Talley Abbey **Ⓒ**, which was founded by Rhys ap Gruffydd, a powerful Welsh prince of the late 12th century. It was a splendid building, 300ft (90m) long and 100 feet (30m) high, and was the only house in Wales belonging to the Premonstratensian Order, which originated in Prémontré, France, in 1119. They were known as the white canons, from their habits, and lived by the order's motto, 'Devotion, learning and service'.

OWAIN GLYNDWR

Caring for the sick and fulfilling parochial duties in the parish, the white canons both farmed and worshipped here for over 300 years. The abbey was badly damaged in Owain Glyndwr's uprising; by the time of the Dissolution, only eight canons remained. They left behind a place of haunting serenity, its ancient walls steeped in prayer and thoughtful meditation.

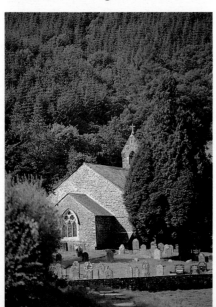

◀ St Michael's Church in Talley was built in the Georgian period in a style reminiscent of the 13th century.

FACT FILE

⚹ Tregaron, 10 miles (16km) north-east of Lampeter, on the A485

▣ Pathfinders 968 (SN 66/76) and 990 (SN 65/75), grid reference SN 680596

miles 0 1 2 3 4 5 6 7 8 9 10 miles
kms 0 1 2 3 4 5 6 7 8 9 10 11 12 13 14 15 kms

◔ Allow 3 to 4 hours, plus another hour if following the nature trail

▭ Clearly defined tracks or tarmac roads. If following the nature trail (permit required), wear waterproof clothing and footwear

P In the square, at the start

▤ The Talbot Hotel in Tregaron

⌘ Welsh Gold Centre open all year, Mon-Fri 9.00am (Sat 9.30am)-5.30pm plus June-Sept, Sun 10am-6pm. Tel. (01974) 298415. Cors Caron Nature Reserve; free permits available with advance notice, Tel. (01974) 831671

I For tourist information, Tel. (01974) 298144

▲ *The route crosses Cors Caron, a peat bog that has been fenced off as a nature reserve. The water shrew (left) lives here and by the river further along the walk, but is prey to owls hunting here.*

Around a peaty nature reserve and an old drovers' town

Tregaron lies on the fringe of the vast wilderness of the Cambrian Mountains. George Borrow (see box on page 122), on his epic tramp through 'Wild Wales' in the 1850s, described it as 'an Andalusian village overhung by its sierra'. The small, unpretentious town is dominated by St Caron's Church, which looms majestically from a domed hillock.

This mound is reputed to be the burial chamber of Caron, the shepherd boy who raised himself through bravery and honesty to become King of Ceredigion in the 3rd century. It was he who gave the town its name — 'Place of Caron'. Tregaron's other famous sons include Twm Shon Cati, a Welsh Robin Hood, and Henry Richard, who founded the Peace Union.

This walk begins in the town square, opposite the Talbot Hotel Ⓐ, where George Borrow experienced 'very good entertainment...an excellent supper and a very comfortable bed'. The 19th-century hotel was originally a drovers' inn. Tregaron was a major centre for stockmen, who converged on the Talbot Arms to refuel body and soul before undertaking the long, hazardous journey across the untamed mountains to the east.

▶ *Tregaron's Talbot Hotel, where the walk begins, was built in the 19th century to cater for drovers.*

THE WALK

TREGARON – CORS CARON

The walk begins from the main square in the centre of Tregaron.

In the centre of the square is a statue **B** of Henry Richard (1812-88), MP for Merthyr Tydfil and an outspoken supporter of disarmament. Born in Tregaron, Richard was apprenticed to a draper before his ordination in 1835. A strong advocate of the disestablishment of the church, he eventually devoted himself to a political career, and founded the European Peace Union, the forerunner of the League of Nations and the United Nations.

The bronze statue, which was unveiled in 1893, portrays a forcible man in a Victorian frock-coat, a sheaf of papers clasped in one hand and his pince-nez in the other.

CELTIC JEWELLERY

On the other side of the square, the route passes the Welsh Gold Centre **C**, where the world-famous Rhiannon range of Celtic silver and gold jewellery is created from Welsh minerals. Tregaron is one of only three places still making specialist jewellery from the dwindling stocks

▼*St Caron's Church in Tregaron, with its battlemented 14th-century tower, overlooks the town from a knoll.*

Nature Reserve **D**, then turn left to Maes-llyn farm.

▶**2** Turn right along the old railway line, which takes you into the reserve. Continue to the observation tower **E**.

▶**3** Either return to the road at Maes-llyn the way you came or, if you have a permit, by turning off to follow the nature trail (waymarked with red-topped posts and red plastic triangles). Retrace your steps along the main road, but then take the first left. Follow this lane uphill towards the distant Cambrian Mountains, until you reach a stone house (Treflyn) on your left. Turn right directly opposite, through a gate onto a farm track. Continue walking, through a second gate, to a T-junction.

▶**1** Leaving the Talbot Hotel **A** behind you, cross the road, passing the Henry Richard statue **B** on your right and the Welsh Gold Centre **C** on your left. Bear left (north-west) along the main street. Cross the bridge and turn right along the B4343. Continue for about 2¼ miles (3.6km), alongside the Cors Caron

▶**4** Turn right along the track. Cross a cattle grid and go straight on through Pen-y-cefn's farmyard onto a surfaced track leading downhill, past Sunnyhill Farm, to a T-junction. Turn left. Return to Tregaron along the main road. Retrace your steps, past St Caron's Church **F** on your right, to the start.

Nature Walk

THE WINGS appear narrow and pointed when the bird is in flight, with a dark band at the tip. The wingbeat is too fast for the pattern on the underwing to be seen clearly.

THE HEAD has the least distinctive markings of any of the birds of prey. The bill is notched for nipping the neck of its live, active prey, which includes birds caught in flight.

THE EGGS are broadly oval and matt buff with a nearly complete covering of reddish spots and blotches. Clutches of 3-5 are laid in May-June.

▲At the route's northern extreme, this observation tower gives wardens and walkers a good view over the reserve.

of Welsh gold. Many of the designs are inspired by the nation's mythology and natural history.

You leave the town on a quiet road sheltered by oak, rowan, beech and hawthorn. The ground rises gently to overlook Cors Caron ❶, or Tregaron Bog, a 4-mile (6.4-km) long raised bog that formed over two large lakes that were impounded behind a glacial moraine.

PLANT SUCCESSION

The habitat gradually altered as the lakes were drained by the Afon Teifi. Open-water plants gave way to reeds, which, in turn, formed dense banks of peat. As the surface dried, alder, birch, oak and pine trees flourished, only to die back when the level of rainfall increased

and the water table was lifted again.

Sphagnum moss carpeted the central area, forming vast accumulations of acid peat and creating three raised bogs, 33 feet (10m) above the original level of the lake beds. Today, the bog is white with cotton grass in summer, and a sea of swaying purple moor-grass by autumn.

END OF THE LINE

You continue along an old railway line across the bog, which is covered with ling, tussocks of deer-grass, bog rosemary, asphodel, tormentil, sundew and lichens. The Teifi cuts through the peat away to the left. Yellow water-lilies float near the banks, together with milfoil, water starwort and pondweed. The river is a valuable habitat for mallard, wigeon, teal and whooper swans.

A high observation tower ❺ gives

▲Part of the route follows a disused railway line, making the going particularly easy. West of the line, the bog (below) stretches across the valley of the Teifi to the hills beyond.

George Borrow

The picture shows a detail of an oil painting of George Borrow by Henry W Phillips. The portrait was painted in 1843, when Borrow's career was just getting started.

George Borrow, destined to become one of the 19th century's most imaginative writers, was born near Norwich in 1808. His family intended for him to be a solicitor, but his passion for adventure and languages led him to travel. He roamed through France, Spain and Germany, mingling with the gipsies, learning their language and falling in love with a romanticized version of their actually less than idyllic lifestyle.

He earned himself wide literary acclaim with the publication of *Gipsies in Spain* (1841) and *The Bible in Spain* (1843).

His subsequent works, *Lavengro* (1851) and *Romany Rye* (1857) were, however, far too outspoken for conservative Victorian tastes; *Lavengro* was branded an 'epic of ale'. Borrow was widely tabooed as the high priest of vulgar taste, and he was never to regain his early popularity.

Wild Wales, published in 1862, attracted little critical attention. It celebrates the author's love of the open road, his spirit for wandering and a rather charming macho Englishness that clearly despised the cultivated humbug of the era.

Borrow ended his days a lonely man, still sensitive to the criticism that destroyed his early fame. He died in 1881. All his works have been re-published several times since his death.

Wild Wales is, perhaps, the most inspired, vividly conjuring up a land of 'the wildest solitudes and most romantic scenery', its narrative coloured with the humour of its native people and Borrow's own unique anecdotal style.

You retrace your steps along the road, then branch off into the hills. Towering high above to your left are the brooding heights of the Cambrian Mountains, where Twm Shon Cati, a favourite villain of Welsh folklore, hid out in his narrow cave. The legend is based on Thomas Jones (c1530-1609), who received an official pardon for some unknown crime in 1559. Down the centuries, many tales have collected around his name; Twm is usually portrayed as a brigand, a highwayman and a talented trickster.

SAINT'S GRAVE

The walk ends back in the town, with a closer look at St Caron's Church ❺. The building stands on an oval mound 24 feet (7.2m) above the road. Legend has it that the earth on which it stands rose up of its own accord to cover St Caron's grave.

The fortified 14th-century tower rises to 60 feet (18m), seemingly out of proportion with the rest of the building. The belfry holds a solitary bell, whose resonant E flat rings out across the parish. Tradition says the original complement of four bells was removed by marauding Irish pirates, though it is more likely they were taken during the Civil War to be smelted down for munitions.

The walk follows the drovers' road back to the square, the heart of this thriving community; as one old drover said to George Borrow about Tregaron, 'Not quite as big as London, but a very good place.'

▶ *As the walk climbs into pastureland, views open out behind you to the distant green hills beyond Cors Caron.*

panoramic views across the bog, where sparrowhawk, merlin and peregrine regularly hunt.

Cors Caron is also the haunt of one of Britain's rarest and most beautiful birds, the red kite. The tributary of the Teifi on the right is a favourite place to spot otters, which feed there on trout.

If you have obtained a permit, you follow a nature trail through the reserve, which is a haven for several butterflies, including the small heath, common blue, green-veined white, peacock and small copper. If you have not, then you walk back along the bed of the old railway line.

DYFED

Explore the countryside around a town in the heart of Wales

The wooded valley of the sparkling River Teifi is a favourite haunt of anglers, who come to pit their skills against the swift-swimming salmon and sea trout. Above it stands the ancient and remote market town of Llandysul. The little town sits in a wedding cake tier of terraces along the river-bank, its predominantly Victorian image preserved in a community that barely caters for the tourist.

The town is famous for preserving many old customs and beliefs. One of the most fiercely Welsh areas of the country, the region inspired one of its sons, Carradoc Evans, to write a collection of stories savagely exposing greed, hypocrisy and corruption in chapel-going communities. Published in 1915, his book *My People* earned him overnight

notoriety and the twin titles of a traitor to his people and 'the most remarkable Welshman of his time'.

The walk begins at St Tysul's Church **Ⓐ**, whose Norman tower rears majestically over the river-bank. In the Dark Ages, pilgrims

▲*Llandysul's impressive 19th-century stone road-bridge was built as a result of some local politics. The snake-like river lamprey (inset), found in the River Teifi, is a blood-sucking parasite. The commemorative lychgate of St Tysul's Church (below left) was built in 1933.*

FACT FILE

❋ Llandysul, 11 miles (17.6km) south-west of Lampeter, on the A486

▱ Pathfinder 1012 (SN 44/54), grid reference SN 418406

miles 0 1 2 3 4 5 6 7 8 9 10 miles
kms 0 1 2 3 4 5 6 7 8 9 10 11 12 13 14 15 kms

◔ Allow 1½ hours

▬ Easy walking on country lanes and footpaths

Ⓟ At the start

🍴 Hotel, pubs and shops in Llandysul

WC At the start

THE WALK

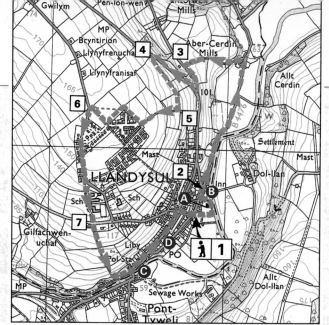

LLANDYSUL

The walk begins from the riverside car park next to the church in Llandysul.

1 Go through the iron gates into the churchyard of St Tysul's **Ⓐ**. Leave through the lychgate and go to the T-junction by the Porth Hotel **Ⓑ**. Turn right along the road.

2 Bear right at the fork, and continue along the lane towards Aber-Cerdin Mills. Just before the old mill, go sharp left through a gate. Follow the track round the farm buildings and uphill to a T-junction with a road.

3 Turn left. At the next junction, turn right. Continue uphill.

4 About 100 paces before the brow of the hill, turn back sharp left onto a grassy path. Go through a kissing-gate and cross two fields, keeping the hedge line to your right. Continue through a gap. Cross the next field with the hedge on your left, to a kissing-gate in the corner.

5 Turn right onto a path between a double hedge. Continue uphill, through a kissing-gate then through a gate onto a road. Turn right. After 20 paces, bear right through a gate onto a footpath between a double hedge. At the end, go through a kissing-gate and left along the road. At the T-junction, turn right. At the end of the road, go through a kissing-gate onto the main road.

6 Turn left. Where the road bends left, just before a school on your right, turn right down the steps. Cross a sports field, making for the kissing-gate in the bottom left-hand corner.

7 Go straight ahead over the road onto a dirt track, downhill. Follow the path to a kissing-gate, then cross the field, keeping the hedge line to your right. Go through a kissing-gate and turn left through a wooded area, alongside the Teifi. At Llandysul Bridge **Ⓒ**, follow the road straight ahead, passing the Gomer Press **Ⓓ**. At a crossroads, turn right to return to the start.

---

crossed the river at the ford where St Tysul (AD462-544) established the first church for the relief of weary travellers. The Normans contributed much to the fabric of the present building, which was later restored by over-zealous Victorians.

Inside, solid pillars and pointed arches lend grandeur to a church that in the 17th century boasted six 'chapels of ease'. A 6th-century stone, set in the north wall, bears the inscription 'Velvor filia Broho' and commemorates Velvoria, the daughter of a Romanized British chief.

The 1933 lychgate celebrates the centenary of Calan-Hen, a festival held in the church for over 150 years. It replaced an annual custom celebrated on the 12th January — New Year's Day in the old Julian calendar — when the men played Cnapan, a game where sticks and clubs were used to knock a ball into the porch of their opponent's church. Injuries and fights were endemic and, in 1833, the clergy sanitized the festival into a Sunday School competition of singing and scripture recital.

FISHERMEN'S REST

The nearby Porth Hotel **Ⓑ** is much frequented by fishermen. Here, generations of travellers have drunk fine ale and dried themselves by blazing log fires after crossing the ford and climbing the old track, which still runs by the hotel.

Through lush green farmland fringed by plump hedgerows, the route follows footpaths and lanes to climb high above the silvery length of the river, which is enclosed by a bank of bright green that in autumn melts to golden yellow as the larch

◀ *In flurries of white water, the River Teifi sweeps down the valley, around massive, moss-covered boulders.*

trees shed their soft needles.

The winding track eventually leads downhill to Llandysul Bridge **Ⓒ**, which dates from the 1850s. It was financed by John Lloyd Davies MP, the scourge of the Rebecca Rioters. The cost of maintaining the previous bridge was met by the parish, which offered the unattractive proposition to Evan Rees, a local mason and publican. A deal was struck; Rees agreed to the proposal, on condition that all future vestry meetings be held in his pub and that his brother would be granted the monopoly of supplying paupers' coffins for the village!

The shops in Llandysul's narrow streets epitomize those of a small town supplying an outlying farming community, and the cattle market is one of the oldest in the country. The people are undeniably proud of their culture. The presses **Ⓓ** of the renowned publishing house Gwasg Gomer specialize in the production and sale of Welsh-interest books. Here, where the existence of the native language was once seriously threatened, there is a passionate and healthy rebirth of a heritage as old and precious as the unspoilt landscape of the Teifi Valley.

INDEX

Abbey Hotel, Llanthony 19, 22
Aber Fellin Bay *85*, 86
Aberaeron 95
Aberaeron harbour 95, *96*
Abercastle 103, *104*
Aberdulais Falls 65–6, 68
Aberdulais Mill (Turner) *68*
Abergavenny *17*, 18
Aberlerry 84
Aberysthwyth 77–8
Aeddan 29
Aeron, River 95
Afon Cothi 117
Afon Dulas 115, *116*
Afon Ffynnon-Ddewi 97
Afon Gwaun 99, *100*
Afon Leri 84
Afon Taf *114*
Afon Teifi *see* Teife, River
Alban Square, Aberaeron 95, *96*
animals
    badger 100, *109*
    dormouse *99*, 100
    fallow deer 25, *71*, 72
    grey seal 75, 76, 87
    horseshoe bat *14*
    otter 43, 99, 122
    Père David's deer 72
    pot-bellied pig 72
    red deer 72
    seal 103
    squirrel 15
    water shrew *119*
    woodmouse *57*
The Argoed 36
Arthur, King 93, 94
Atlantic College 59, *60*

Baldwin, Archbishop 11, 12, 29
Bannau, Sir Gaer 101, *102*
Barafundle Bay 74
de Barri family 105, 108
beaches
    Borth *84*
    Rhossili Bay 63
Bedd Arthur 92–3, *94*
Beddau'r Derwyddon 110
Bell Inn 41, *42*
Berw-ddu waterfall 52
Bettws Newydd church 29–30
bird sanctuaries
    Ramsey Island 75
    Worms Head 63
birds
    Afon Teife 121
    bar-tailed godwit *79*
    Black Mountains 14
    buzzard 43, 100, 110
    Carreg Cennen 109
    chough *87*
    cormorant 95

curlew *19*
Dare Valley 51–2
fulmar 103
greater spotted woodpecker *12*
guillemot *63*
gulls 95
house martin 95
jackdaw *23*
Llanthony Valley 22
Manorbier 107
merlin 121
Mount Pleasant Wood 116
Pembrokeshire coast 85
peregrine falcon 101, 106
pheasant *49*
raptors 101, 122
raven 100, 110
red kite 101, 110, 122
reed warbler *61*
short-eared owl 110
Talley Lakes 118
thrush *45*
waders 82
whinchat *15*, 22
woodcock 100
woodpecker 51
Bishops Bridge *see* Pont Escob
Black Mountain 110
Black Mountains 11–14
Blaenavon 16, 18
Blorenge mountain 15, *17*
Boat House, Laugharne 112, *113*
The Boat Inn 35, *36*
Borrow, George 119, 122
Borth beach *84*
Bosherston 73, 74
Bosherston church 73, 74
Bosherston Ponds 73, 74
Brecon and Abergavenny Canal 15,
    16, *31*, 32
Brecon Beacons *54*
Brecon Beacons National Park 11–22
Broad Haven 74
Bronze Age cairns 92
Brunel, I.K. 53, 54
Brynffynnon Hotel 45, *46*
Buck Stone 25, *26*
Burges, William 57
burial mounds
    Garth Hill 47, *48*
    King's Quoit 107
    Rhossili Down 64
    Tregaron 119
The Bush Inn, Penallt 35, *36*
Bute, Marquess of 54
Bute, 3rd Marquess of 57
butterflies
    comma 117
    Cors Caron 122
    Cwmtydu 97
    fritillaries *25*, 117

speckled wood 117
Bwllfa Dare Colliery 52, 54

Cairns 21
    Bronze Age 75
    pre-Roman 53
Cambrian Mountains 122
Camera Obscura 77, *78*
canals
    Brecon and Abergavenny 15, 16,
        31, 32
    history 17
    transport system 17–18
Candleston Castle *49*, 50
Cardigan 78–80
Cardigan Castle 80, 81, *82*
Cardigan Island 82
Careg Sampson *see* Sampson's
    Stone
Carn Arthur 93, *94*
Carn Menyn 92
Carn Sian 93, *94*
Carreg Cennen 109, 110
Carreg Cennen Castle 109, 110
Carreg Gybi 88, *90*
Carregwastad Point *85*, 86
Castell Allt-goch 116
Castell Bâch 97–8
Castell Coch 48, 57, *58*
Castell-coch 103, *104*
Castle Mill 42, 43
castles
    Candleston *49*, 50
    Cardigan 80, 81, *82*
    Carreg Cennen 109, 110
    Castell Coch 48, 57, *58*
    Clytha 27
    Laugharne 111–12, *113*
    Manorbier 105, *106*
    Margam 72
    Pen-coed 37, 38, *39*
    Penhow 37, 38, 39, *40*
    Red Castle *see* Castell Coch
    St Donat's 59, *60*
    Skenfrith 42, 43, *44*
    Welsh Marches 44
Cati, Twm Shon 119, 122
caves 70
Celtic field system 104
Celtic hillforts 108, 116
Ceredigion Museum 77, *78*
Cerrig Meibion Arthur 93, *94*
Chapel of St John the Baptist 42, 43–4
charcoal burning 11, 14
Charles, Prince of Wales 77–8
Church of St Tysilio 98
Cliff Railway 77, *78*
cliffs 88, *90*, 103
Clytha Arms 27
Clytha Castle 27–8
coal mining, Cwmdare 54

Coastguard Station, Dinas Mawr 88, 90
Coed Morgannwg Way 51, 52
Coed Wen 38, 39
Coed y Bwnydd fort 28–9
Cors Caron 120, 121
Cosmeston 62
Cosmeston Lakes Country Park 62
Coxe, Archdeacon 28–9
Craig Gwladys Woodlands 66–7
cromlechs, Careg Sampson 103, 104
Culver Hole 69, 70
Cwm Col-huw 56
Cwmdare 51–3
Cwmtydu 97, 98
Cwmyoy church 12, 13–14
Cwmyoy village 11

Dan Beard wreck 88, 90
Dare, River 51, 53–4
Dare Valley Country Park 51, 52, 54
Din Geraint fort 81, 82
Dinas Mawr 88, 89
dovecot, Manorbier 106, 107
Dulais, River 68
Dyffryn Arms, Pontfaen 99, 100
Dylan's Walk 112, 113

Eagles' Nest viewpoint 23
Edwinsford 117–18
Edwinsford Arms 118
Eglwys Llandysiliogogo see Church
  of St Tysilio
eisteddfods 82
Emrys, Dewi, memorial 89
Evans, Carrodoc 123

Fenton, Richard 76
Fforest Coal Pit 11, 12
field systems 63, 104
First Try (Gordon Young) 71
fish 81
  carp 15
  dab 111
  eel 102
  gudgeon 47
  lamprey 65, 123
  pike 117, 118
  roach 15
Foeldrygarn 91, 92, 94
forts 56, 108, 116
  see also Iron Age forts
Foxhole Slade 70
French invasion memorial 85–6

Gaer Hill 24
Gaers 30
Gardwnda 86
Garn Fawr 87, 88
Garth Hill 47, 48
Geoffrey of Monmouth 93, 94
Gerald of Wales 105
Giraldus Cambrensis 105

Glamorgan Heritage Coastal Path 59,
  60
Glyndwr, Owain 63, 82, 110, 118
Goat's Hole Cave 70
Golden Road 92
Gomer Press 124
Goodwick 85–6
Govilon 16, 17
Gower peninsula 63–4
Grwyne Fawr valley 11, 12
Guto see Morgan, Griffith
Guto's Grave 45, 46
Gwaun Valley 99, 100

Hall, Mr and Mrs S.C. 68
Harbour Village, Goodwick 86
Hatterrall Ridge 19, 20, 21
Hearst, William Randolph 60
Helvetia wreck 63, 64
Hen Eglwys 72
Henfynyw church 96
Highmeadow Woods 25
Hill family 17, 18
hill forts 108, 116
Holy Well of St Patricio 12
Honddu, River 12, 19

Industry, South Wales 68
insects, snipe fly 37
Iron Age forts
  Castell Bâch 97–8
  Castell-coch 103, 104
  Coed y Bwnydd 28–9
  Din Geraint 81, 82
  Dinas Mawr 88, 89
  Gaer Hill 24
  history 30
  Lampeter 115
  Mynydd y Castell 71, 72
  Pen Dinas 77
  Stackpole 73, 74
  Wilcrick Hill 39
iron workings 23, 24

Jellyfish 83
Jones, Rev. Thomas Alban 95
Jones, Thomas 122
Jones, William 27–8

King's Quoit 107

Lakes
  Bosherston 73
  Cosmeston 62
  Llyn y Fan Fach 101, 102
  Llyn y Fan Fawr 102
Lampeter 115, 116
Landor, Walter Savage 20, 22
Laugharne 111, 112
Laugharne Castle 111–12, 113
lava cliffs 88, 90
Lavernock 61–2

ley lines 94
Liberty Ships 90
lifeboat stations
  Fishguard 85, 86
  St David's 75, 76
lighthouses
  Nash Point 60
  Ynys Meicel 88, 89
limekilns 67, 98, 109, 110
Llanddeusant 101, 102
Llandysul 123, 124
Llandysul Bridge 124
Llanfoist 15, 16, 17, 18
Llanthony Priory 19–21, 22
Llantwit Major 55, 56
Llanwonno 45–6
Llanwonno church 45, 46
Llanwonno Forest 45, 46
Llewellyn family 54
Lloyd Davies, John 124
Llygad Llwchwr see Loughor, River
Llyn y Fan Fach lake 101, 102
long distance paths
  Coed Morgannwg Way 51, 52
  Glamorgan Heritage Coastal Path 59,
    60
  Offa's Dyke Path 20, 21
  Pembrokeshire Coast Path 73, 74,
    81, 86, 88, 91, 103, 107
  Ridgeway Walk 48
  Usk Valley Walk 27, 29–30
  Wye Valley Walk 23, 24, 33
Longhole Cave 70
Longhouse Farm 104
Loughor, River 109, 110
Lower Wye Valley 23
Lucas, John 69

Mackworth, Lady Molly 31
Maelgwn Gwynedd 84
Magor 37–9
Maiden Castle, Devon 30
mammals see animals
Manor Wood 33, 34
Manorbier 105, 106
Manorbier Bay 107
Manorbier Castle 105, 106
Marcher Earls 44
Marconi plaque 62
Marcross 59–60
Marcross church 59, 60
Margam Abbey Church 71, 72
Margam Castle 72
Margam Country Park 71, 72
Margam Stones Museum 72
maze, Margam 72
medieval pillow mounds 110
medieval village, Cosmeston 62
memorial, French invasion 85–6
Merthyr Mawr 49, 50
Mill House 33, 34
millstones 35

mine workings 67
mink *41*, 43
Monnow, River 42, 43, 44
Monnow Valley 41–4
Morgan, Griffith 46
motte and bailey 116
Mount Pleasant Wood 116
Mynachlog-ddu 93
Mynydd y Castell fort *71*, 72

Nant Melyn 102
Nash Point 60
National Library of Wales 78
national parks 11–22, 75–6
National Trust visitor centre, Rhossili 63, 64
nature reserves
    Cardigan Island 82
    Carreg Cennen 109
    Coed Wen 39
    Cors Caron 120, 121
    Longhole Cave 70
    Talley Lakes 118
    Ynyslas 83–4
nature walks 21, 89, 121
Near Hearkening Rock 26
Neath, industrial landscape 68
Needle Rock 85
Neolithic burial chamber, Gardwnda 86

Offa's Dyke Path 20, 21
Old Castle Head 106, 108
Orangery, Margam 71–2
Overton Mere 69

Paper mills 33
Partrishow church 12–13, *14*
Paviland Cave 70
Pembrokeshire Coast Path 73, 74, *81*, 86, 88, 91, 103, 107
Pembrokeshire National Park 75–6
Pen Anglas 85, 86
Pen Dinas fort 77
Pen-coed Castle 37, 38, 39
Pen-twyn 36
Penallt 35
Penallt Old Church 35, 36
Penarth 61, 62
Penhow Castle 37, 38, 39, 40
Penhow church 38, 39, 40
Penscynor Wild Life Park 66
Penterry church 23, 24
Perrot, Sir John 112, 114
Perry-Herrick, Sophie 39
petrified forest 84
piers, Penarth 61, 62
Pont Escob 11, 13
Pontfaen *99*, 100
Pontymoel Basin 32
Pontypool Folly 32
Pontypool Park Gates 31, 32
Pontypool Park Grotto 31, 32

Port-Eynon 69, 70
Porth Hotel 124
prehistoric settlement 53
Preseli Hills 91
Presipe bay *108*
Priests Nose 106, 107
Procurator's House, Magor 37, 38
Punchbowl, the 16, 18
Pwll Arian 88, 89
Pwll Deri 88, 90

Railways
    Dare Aman 54
    disused 121, 122
    Merthyr, Tredegar and Abergavenny 17
    Taff Vale 54
    tramway 17–18
    Vale of Rheidol Narrow Gauge Steam Railway 78
Ramsey Island 75, 76
Red Book of Hergest 101
Red Castle *see* Castell Coch
Rees, Evan 124
Rhiw Cwrw 20, 21
Rhizostoma 83
Rhondda, Lord 39
Rhossili 63, 64
Rhossili Down 64
Rhossili Hill Beacon 64
Rhosson Farm 75, 76
ap Rhys, Gruffyd 81, 82, 110, 112, 118
Richard, Henry 120
Ridgeway Walk 48
Roche Castle 112, 114
rocks
    Buck Stone 25, 26
    Near Hearkening Rock 26
    stacks 89
    Suck Stone 26
roodscreen, Bettws Newydd 29

St Bride's Church 37, 38, 40
St Bride's Netherwent 38, 40
St Bridget's Church *41*, 43
St Caron's Church 119, 120, 121
St David 19, 21, 76
St David's 76
St David's Church, Llanthony 20, 21
St David's University College 115, 116
St Dogmaels abbey 81
St Donat's Castle *59*, 60
St Donat's Church 60
St Gwyndaf's Church 86
St Gwynno's Forest 45
St Illtud 55, 56
St James's Church, Manorbier 106, 108
St Justinian's Chapel 75, 76
St Martin's Church, Laugharne 112, 113
St Mary's Church 37, 38
St Maughan's Church 42, 44
St Maur family 40

St Michael's Church, Talley 118
St Patricio 12
St Sampson 104
St Teilo Church 49
St Tysul 123, 124
Salisbury Farm 38, 40
Salt House 69, 70
Salus wreck 88, 90
Sampson's Stone 103, 104
sand dunes
    Cardigan 80, 82
    Tythegston 49, 50
    Ynyslas 83
Sea Aquarium, Aberaeron 96
Sea View 112, 114
'The Sharple' 20, 22
Shaw, George Bernard 106
shipping, Cardigan 79, 81
Silian, Prince (later Saint) 55–6
Sir John's Hill 112, 114
Site of Special Scientific Interest, Gwaun Valley 99
Skenfrith 41, 42, 44
Skenfrith Castle 42, 43, 44
smugglers 69, 97
snakes, adders *59*
Stackpole Court 73, 74
Stackpole Quay 73, 74
Stackpole village 73, 74
standing stones, Carn Menyn 92–3, 94
Staunton 25, 26
stone quarries 35, 36
Stonehenge 92–4
Stones Museum, Margam 72
Stradling family 60
Strumble Head 87
Suck Stone 26
Sweyne's Houses 64

Taff Gorge 48
Taff, River 47, 48
Taff's Well 47, 48
Taff's Well Inn 47, 48
Talbot, Christopher Rice Mansel 72
Talbot Hotel, Tregaron 119, 120
Talley 117
Talley Abbey 117, 118
Talley Lakes 117, 118
Tarren y Bwllfa 52, *53*
Taylor, Mrs Margaret 112, 113
Teife, River 80, 81–2, 115, 116, 121, 123, 124
The 365 Steps 23, 24
Thomas, Dr Herbert 93
Thomas, Dylan 111, 112, 113–14
Thomas, Margaret Haig 39
Traeth Maelgwyn 83, 84
tramways 16, 17–18
transport system 17, 18
Travellers Rest pub 57
Tredegar and Abergavenny Railway 17
trees, Gwaun Valley 100

Tregaron 119
Tregaron Bog 121
Tregate Bridge 42, 44
Trelleck 34
Tresilian Bay 55
Tresilian Cave 55, 56
Trevine 103, 104
Turner, J.M.W. *68*
Twrch Trwyth 94
Twrch valley 101, 102
Tysilio, Saints 98
Tythegston 49, 50

*U*nder Milk Wood (Dylan Thomas)
  111, 113 114
University of Aberysthwyth 77–8
Usk, River 29
Usk Valley 18, 27
Usk Valley Walk 27, 29–30

*V*ale of Ewyas 19, 22
Vale of Neath 67, 68
Vale of Rheidol Narrow Gauge Steam
  Railway 78
Vaughan Thomas, Wynford 89
viaduct, Brunel's 53, 54
viel field system 63
Virtuous Well 34

*W*alls, dry stone 67
war memorial, Magor 38, 39
Warrior Stone 92
Watkins, Alfred 94
Waverley paddle steamer 61
Welsh Gold Centre 119, 120–1
Welsh Marches, castles 44
wharves 16, 17
White Brook 33
white canons 118
White Horse Inn, Staunton 25, 26
Whitebrook Valley 33, 34
Wilcrick Hill fort 39
wild flowers
  arrowhead *31*
  bluebell 27, 39
  centaury 87
  cherry *35*
  Coed Wen 39
  creeping buttercup 52
  gorse *97*
  hedge woundwort *115*
  Laugharne 114
  lichen 89
  Llanfair Clydogau 116
  Manorbier 107
  marsh thistle *51*, 52
  Pembrokeshire Coast Path 76
  red valerian *95*
  rock samphire *103*
  sea bindweed 49
  sea campion *77*
  sea kale *105*

sea lavender *73*
snake's head fritillary 107
sneezewort *91*
spotted orchid 109
star sedge 52
Strumble Head 87
tree mallow *69*, 103
Tregaron Bog 121
viper's bugloss 49
water-crowfoot *101*
water-lily 73, 118, 121
Wild Wales (George Borrow) 122
wildlife, Brecon and Abergavenny
  Canal 32
wildlife park, Cardigan *81*
woodland walk, Wye Valley 33–4
woodlands, Craig Gwladys 66–7
Woolf, Virginia 106–7
Worms Head 63, 64
wrecks
  Dan Beard 88, 90
  Helvetia 63, 64
  Needle Rock 85, 86
  Rhossili Bay 63–4
  Salus 88, 90
Wye Gorge 35
Wye, River 23, 35
Wye Valley 23
Wye Valley Walk 23, 24, 33
Wyndcliff 23, 24

*Y*nys y Castell 103, 104
Ynyslas 83–4
Ynysybwl 45
Ynysybwl church 45
Young, Gordon, *First Try 71*

PICTURE CREDITS

All map artwork, MC Picture Library;
AA Picture Library: 14tr; Caroline Bacon:
51t, 52bl, 53tl, 53tr, 53bl, 54, 54cl, 54b; Jim
Bain/NHPA: 75c; Chris Barber: 11t, 14tl,
16cr, 18tr, 21cl, 22bl; Janet and Colin
Board/Wales Scene: 22br, 76bl,108b;
John Buckingham/NHPA: 12bl, 103l (Inset);
Cadw Welsh Historical Monuments: 57t,
57br, 58br; L Campbell/Scotland in Focus:
97t (Inset); Laurie Campbell/NHPA: 19t
(Inset), 23t (Inset), 63t (Inset); Vanessa
Cawley/MC Picture Library: 58bl; Celtic
Picture Library: 11t (Inset), 13b, 21br,
63br, 75b, 77t, 77br, 78b, 85t; Hugh
Clarke/Nature Photographers Ltd: 109t
(Inset); Andrew Cleave/Nature
Photographers Ltd: 115t (Inset);Eric
Crichton/Bruce Coleman: 33b; Stephen
Dalton/NHPA: 45t (Inset), 57t (Inset),
79b, 95tl, 99t (Inset), 119t (Inset); Robert
Eames: 41t, 41b, 43tr, 43cl, 43b, 44tr, 44cl,
44b, 63t, 64bl, 73t, 73cl, 73br; Jonathan
Eastland/Ajax News and Feature Service:
90bl; English Heritage Photo Library: 30cr;
Paul Felix: 11br, 23b, 24br, 35t, 36b; Derek
Foss: 76br; Bob Gibbons/Natural Image:
65br; Jeff Goodman/NHPA: 47cr; Ray
Granger: 61t, 61b, 62bl; Jean Hall/Nature
Photographers Ltd: 83t (Inset); A R
Hamblin/Frank Lane Picture Library: 15t (Inset);
Brian Hawkes/NHPA: 105t (Inset); Richard
Hayman/National Trust/Aberdulais
Falls: 68cl;E A Janes/NHPA: 69t
(Inset); Martin King/Swift Picture
Library: 77t (Inset); Geoffrey Kinns/
Biofotos: 14c; J Lawton Roberts/Aquila: 87t
(Inset); Michael Leach/NHPA: 49tl, 71cr;
Mansell Collection: 18c, 22tl; Mary Evans
Picture Library: 14b, 121t; S and O Mathews:
75tl; MC Picture Library: 89l, 122l; George
McCarthy: 59t (Inset); Duncan McEwan/
Aquila: 37t (Inset); Lutra/NHPA: 117t
(Inset); Colin Molineux: 25tl, 26bl, 26br,
33t, 34bl; Jeremy Moore: 79t, 81t, 81r, 81b,
83t, 83b, 84bl, 87t, 89tr, 89b, 90tl, 90tr,
90br, 91t, 92b, 93tr, 93b, 94t, 94b, 95tr, 96b,
97t, 98bl, 99t, 100c, 100bl, 106b, 107t,
107cr, 107b, 108t, 108l; National Library
of Wales: 82bl; National Maritime
Museum: 85t (Inset); National Museum
of Wales, Cardiff/Bridgeman Art Library:
114t; NHPA: 41t (Inset); Penhow Castle:
40cl; Richard Phipps/MC Picture
Library: 21tr; Derek Pratt: 15t; Derek
Pratt/Waterways Photo Library: 15cl,
15br, 16t, 16bl, 18bl; HansReinhard/
Bruce Coleman: 91t (Inset); Jason
Smalley: 37t, 37b, 39t, 39cr, 39b, 40tr,
114bl, 115b, 117bl, 118bl, 119t, 116bl,
117t, 115t, 40b, 109t, 110b, 111l, 113tl,
113t, 113bl, 113br, 119br, 120br, 121b,
122t, 122cr, 122b, 123t, 123b, 124bl;
Sorensen and Olsen/NHPA: 61t (Inset);
Paul Sterry/Nature Photographers: 51t
(Inset), 123t(Inset); M J Thomas/Celtic
Picture Library: 74bl; Roger Tidman/
Nature Photographers: 35t (Inset); Roger
Viltos: 69t, 70b, 71t, 72cl, 72b, 101t, 101bl,
102bl, 103t, 104cl, 104b, 105t; Wales Tourist
Board: 23t; Roy Waller/NHPA: 111tr; The
Wernher Collection: 68b; Tony Wharton/
Frank Lane Picture Agency: 25tr; Harry
Williams: 27t, 27bl, 29tl, 29tr, 29b, 30tl,
30bl, 31t, 32cr, 32b, 45t, 46b, 47t, 47bl,
48br, 49tr, 50b, 55t, 55b, 56b, 59t, 59b, 60b,
65tr, 66bl, 66br, 67t, 67c, 67b, 68t; Tim
Woodcock: 19t, 22tr; David Woodfall/
NHPA: 27t (Inset), 31b, 73t (Inset).